Realistic Railroading with Toy Trains

Joe Lesser and Pete Youngblood
Photography by Joe Lesser, unless otherwise noted

GREENBERG BOOKS

A Division of Kalmbach Publishing Co.

The Authors

Pete and Joe and their handiwork, the JL/ATSF Railway. William Garnet photo

JOE AND HIS BROTHER'S new Lionel train set, given to them in 1951, contained the classic 773 Hudson locomotive. Finding the words "Lionel Lines" stamped on its tender an unrealistic annoyance, they used steel wool to remove the offending words and happily renumbered both tender and locomotive to more closely match the prototypical Santa Fe 4-6-4s.

When Joe isn't too busy with his model railroad activities, as president of J. K. Lesser Productions he produces business and industrial videotapes for marketing, sales, and training. He has owned and operated this business for more than 30 years.

PETER'S INTEREST in trains dates to childhood and his brother's Lionel set. Unhappy with the clean, shiny finish of the engines and cars, he took them outdoors and soaked them in real water and dirt in a less-than-successful attempt to make them look more realistic.

A former military and commercial pilot now working in film and television as writer/producer, technical consultant, and narrator, Peter still flies for fun and keeps his flight instructor's rating current. He is the author of the book *Modeling Cajon*, published in 1985 by Trans-Anglo Press (now Pentrex). Without a layout at present, he custom-paints model locomotives and rolling stock in his spare time.

Art director and cover design: Kristi Ludwig
Designer: Mike Schafer

Publisher's Cataloging in Publication
   Lesser, Joe.
       Realistic railroading with toy trains / by Joe Lesser and
     Pete Youngblood.
       p. cm.
       ISBN 0-89778-399-9

     1. Railroads—Model. I. Youngblood, Pete. II. Title.
  TF197.L48 1995   625.1'9
                QBI95-20253

Contents

Foreword

I'VE BEEN FASCINATED with trains all my life. Born and raised in Los Angeles, California, I was constantly aware of railroads—the Santa Fe, Southern Pacific, and Union Pacific. These lines were the big three railroads moving freight and passengers in and out of the city during the years I was growing up.

My favorites were the red and silver Santa Fe "Warbonnet" diesels and the gleaming stainless steel passenger trains they pulled. So impressive were they that the second train my brother and I bought was the Lionel *Super Chief*, the same set that still operates on the JL/ATSF Railway today.

From 1950, when we got our first train set, to 1986, I continued to accumulate Lionel trains, but it had been years since I'd had the original layout on which to operate them. This situation, however, changed suddenly.

First and rather incredibly, my mother-in-law and my wife, Jo Ann, suggested that I think about building a layout in our living room! Lots of space would remain for socializing, they theorized, and besides, wouldn't it be fun to entertain guests with a train layout and let them rekindle nostalgic memories that could be shared with ours? Only a fool would argue with such an offer! I quickly agreed it was a great idea.

Second, and at about that same time, I also had the good fortune of meeting Peter Youngblood, a fellow model railroader who shared interest both in the southwestern United States and the Santa Fe Railway.

Peter's conviction and talent soon convinced me to consider constructing a layout in which trains could move through realistic scenery and highly detailed mini-scenes. This concept, somewhat ambitious by conventional three-rail thinking in 1986, became a natural path toward "Hi-railing," a term used contemporarily to denote toy train operators who combine scale and non-scale three-rail trains with a conscious effort to achieve greater realism.

Our interest in prototype modeling and operation probably can be traced to the fact that we began running Lionel trains in our teenage years and looked upon those trains as more than toys. I suppose we would have liked to run real trains in our backyards, but that being impossible, we opted for miniatures, using the real ones for inspiration.

O gauge ready-to-run trains with smoke, whistles, and horns captured my imagination; Peter changed to the smaller HO ("Half O") gauge, preferring its scale exactness and the challenge of building locomotives, rolling stock, and structures. The so-named JL/ATSF Railway brought these interests together so that we might construct a Hi-rail railroad based on the prototype Santa Fe Railway.

We began the design stage of the layout in June of 1986 and started benchwork three months later. Over the next six years we spent almost every Wednesday night working on the railroad into the early morning hours. Many Saturdays were also set aside for longer sessions. Working together as we did always proved challenging and tremendously satisfying.

The golden spike was driven and the layout "finished" in 1991. Now the JL/ATSF Railway serves as a continuing source of operating pleasure for adults and of fun and inspiration to kids. And there are always subtle improvements that keep us busy.

The intent of this book, therefore, is to share with you the experiences and techniques we used to create and build a highly detailed prototypical Hi-rail layout.

ALL ABOARD!

—*Joe Lesser*

1 Considering the Prototype

TO MODEL RAILROADERS, the word "prototype" has a unique meaning that goes beyond its definition as "an original model on which something is patterned." In the hobby—and in this book—when we refer to "the prototype" we're talking about the real railroad and its environment: the cars and locomotives, the track, the ties, the operation, the geography, the topography. In fact, for many in the hobby, the ultimate goal is to build a realistic model of the prototype and to run the trains just like the real thing.

Some hobbyists, known as "scale" modelers, started out with the popular smaller HO or N scale trains, which by definition are highly detailed accurate representations of prototype locomotives and cars. In general, they have stuck to that principle of scale accuracy in building their model railroads.

At the opposite end of the model railroading spectrum are the toy train hobbyists. Some simply collect Lionel, American Flyer, Marx, and other

"Toy trains? Wow! Looks like the real thing!" That would be the greatest compliment authors Lesser and Youngblood could receive. The object of building a Hi-rail layout is, after all, to make toy trains look as much like the real thing as possible.

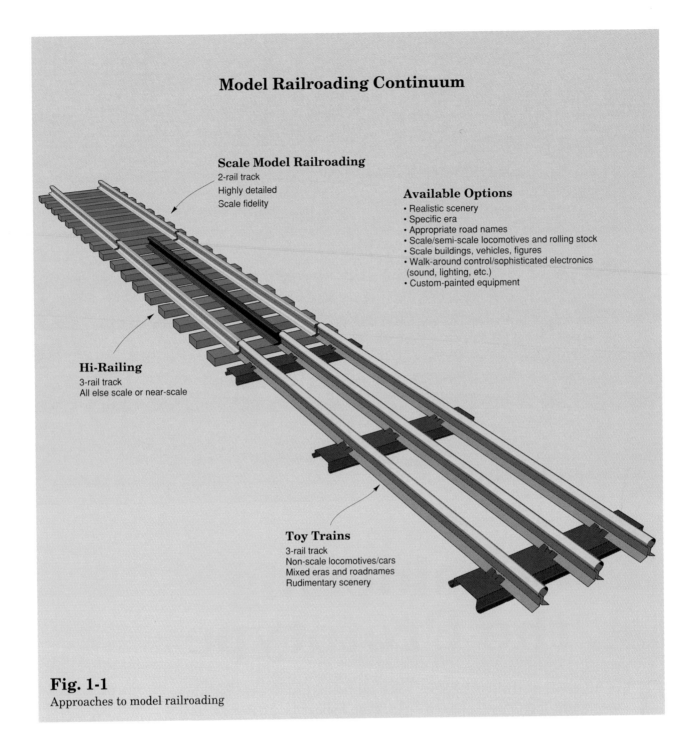

Model Railroading Continuum

Scale Model Railroading
2-rail track
Highly detailed
Scale fidelity

Available Options
• Realistic scenery
• Specific era
• Appropriate road names
• Scale/semi-scale locomotives and rolling stock
• Scale buildings, vehicles, figures
• Walk-around control/sophisticated electronics (sound, lighting, etc.)
• Custom-painted equipment

Hi-Railing
3-rail track
All else scale or near-scale

Toy Trains
3-rail track
Non-scale locomotives/cars
Mixed eras and roadnames
Rudimentary scenery

Fig. 1-1
Approaches to model railroading

trains made since the turn of the century, and some build the toy train version of a layout: track and accessories on a flat sheet of plywood.

Many others entered the hobby in the late 1940s or 1950s with toy trains—again, usually Lionel, American Flyer, or Marx—and continue to purchase toy train equipment as adults. But, because of their interest in the prototype, they have taken a slightly different approach toward scale modeling. It's really an amalgamation of the two approaches to model railroading and it's called "Hi-railing" (in reference to the more unrealistic, taller profile of toy train track). In short, Hi-railing is scale modeling with toy trains. That's what this book is about.

Interestingly, within this approach to the hobby, there are degrees of Hi-railing. The accompanying diagram (fig. 1-1) illustrates the point. At the far left of the toy train continuum are those who follow the traditional approach described above. You can become a Hi-railer at any point or participate to any degree. For example, you can pick a prototype to model—Santa Fe, for instance—and build a layout that runs only Santa Fe locomotives and rolling stock (and those of other appropriate regional roads). Maybe your objective is to duplicate a particular geographic area, or a specific mountain range, prairie, river, harbor, city, village. Modeling that particular faithfully is an aspect of Hi-railing. You can also create a generic prototype that has all of the realism but doesn't follow any specific prototype.

How about the kinds of trains you'll be running on the layout? Which era are you going to model? The Wild West of the late 1800s? The steam-diesel transition period of the 1940s and '50s? The modern era? Or no particular time? What season are you going to depict? We've even seen a terrific Hi-rail layout that has an overall summery appearance, but around a bend on the back side of the layout there's a stark wintry scene with a frozen river, bare trees, and snow all around!

At each point in the continuum, you can come as close to or stray as far from the prototype in your modeling as you choose. If you desire to go as far as you can toward prototype accuracy (given the limitations of three-rail track and the concessions you have to make with rolling stock), you'll select a railroad and a segment of it to model, then duplicate its geographic location and topographic appearance with recognizable scenes,

and finally model and operate a portion of the equipment used there during the specific era you've chosen. That is the ultimate in Hi-rail realism; it's up to you to decide how far you want to go toward scale modeling.

Staying within these parameters will automatically enhance the realism of your modeling, yet nothing prevents you from suddenly changing reality to accommodate a particular locomotive, car, or accessory that's a "gotta have." Working toward greater realism doesn't mean you can't bend the rules. It's your railroad and you're the president of the company!

There are additional factors to consider when choosing a prototype to model. For example, if your interests run parallel to what's already available from model train manufacturers, so much the better—but if they're different, don't despair. Much of what is available at any given time can be modified, repainted, and relettered to look very realistic on your layout.

Don't overlook the possibility of creating your own fictional railroad to model. Many modelers have based their train layouts on a combination of real railroads by incorporating the favorite elements of each. The result is often a convincing imaginary prototype composite railroad.

Many times where you live is a good choice for the geographic setting, and your daily travels give you ample opportunity to visualize your area in model form. Or maybe you'd like to model the region you lived in as a child. Nostalgia is the key ingredient in many of the more realistic layouts, and it's fun to turn back the clock.

Within a particular geographic setting you can also observe specific railroad operations, but if you choose to model a time in the past, you have the additional challenge of doing research to see what something

The San Gabriel mountain range as seen from the Santa Fe main line at Summit in Cajon Pass.

looked like that is no longer there.

The JL/ATSF Railway prototype is based on a combination of all of these things. The rest of this book describes the process we went through in designing and building the layout; we hope it will give you a better idea of what lies ahead should you choose to become a Hi-railer.

CHOICE OF RAILROAD

Fascinated by the history of the Atchison, Topeka & Santa Fe Railway in developing the West; its colorful association with Native Americans of the southwestern United States; its famous passenger trains like the *Super Chief*, powered by sleek red and silver "Warbonnet" diesels; and the fact that Lionel Santa Fe equipment was readily available made this prototype a logical choice.

A secondary interest was in the Southern Pacific Railroad, also a railroad with a colorful historical influence on the development of California and the Southwest. Both interests came about naturally as we live in Santa Fe-land, Southern California, and rode and saw those trains as children. Nostalgia, familiarity, and fond recollections of a time gone by influenced our choice. There was never really any other choice.

Photos taken from the period you are modeling are an invaluable source of information. In the case of the photo of the Santa Fe streamliner passing beneath a cantilever signal at Devore, California, we get a good look at the locomotive, the right-of-way, the scenery, the signal, and—by virtue of the maintenance man on the bridge—an excellent idea of the relative scale. Santa Fe photo

GEOGRAPHIC LOCATION AND ERA

Our second decision was to choose a geographic location on the Santa Fe and an era we wished to depict. A location familiar to both of us extends from San Bernardino westward to the outskirts of Pasadena, an actual distance of 30 miles.

This area offers a dramatic contrast between a flat, rather arid valley through which the railroad runs and a mountain range whose peaks reach 10,000 feet in the immediate background to the north. If the steep mountains were depicted on a painted backdrop, then we would still be able to model the less-severe mainline grades of the foothills in combination with the flat stretch of valley. As it turned out, we had to greatly condense and slightly fictionalize the prototype location to fit the space available to us.

Finally, we had to decide the era we would model on the layout. A number of diesel and steam locomotives were already on the roster, so we locked onto the Transition Era, when steam locomotives were running side-by-side with diesels. Everything on the layout from the trains to automobiles and buildings were to look as they did back then.

RESEARCHING THE PROTOTYPE

Part of the enjoyment of modeling a railroad from a bygone era is compiling photos of everyday details. Often a photo shows a lot more than just the main subject (i.e., locomotive, rolling stock, freight yard, turntable). Careful study of old photos often reveals a multitude of details, including signals, right-of-way signs, and the relative scale size of objects, determined by people working or standing beside them.

If you live reasonably close to your chosen prototype, you have the advantage of being able to take photographs of it. Take lots of them for later study and reference. It's amazing what you'll find as you discover where to look; it's a visual challenge that will consistently help you achieve greater realism.

Books and magazines loaded with photographs, railroad historical societies (*Model Railroader* Magazine publishes a list of them every February), videos, railroad collectible shows, visiting other layouts—all are excellent sources for prototype research and information. Lucky we are that America's railroad history has been so thoroughly documented!

Having chosen a prototype, research it. You'll be impressed by what you learn that will find practical application time and again.

How did we name the railroad? It never occurred to us that it would be called anything other than Atchison, Topeka & Santa Fe, but adding JL gives the JL/ATSF a special identity and personality. JL stands for Jo Ann Lesser, who was instrumental in starting the layout and supportive while we built it.

Joe and Jo Ann Lesser at the mainline control panel of the JL (for Jo Ann Lesser)/ATSF Railway. William Garnet photo

2 Layout Concept and Design

WHERE TO BUILD the layout will be one of your first considerations. Those fortunate enough to have warm, dry, empty basements are blessed. Heated and air-conditioned attics are appropriate, if you can stand erect in them. Garages are acceptable if you can control the temperature and keep down the dust and dirt. In short, select a place for your layout where both you and your trains can be comfortable.

Where we live, basements are few and far between, and so model railroads are often built in garages. Cars occupy the Lesser garage, so that

didn't leave much in the way of alternatives. Where could we build a railroad? Jo Ann suggested we build it—believe it or not—in the living room! It took us a while to determine if she was really serious; she was. The layout we envisioned would best fit into an L-shaped area. It all seemed logical once we started sketching various track plans.

The living room turned out to be an excellent choice for the layout, although when we started construction we couldn't visualize how dramatic the finished layout would appear. Nor could we have imagined that it would

One of the layout builder's first decisions is where to build the layout. Most model railroaders think in terms of basement or garage. Joe and Jo Ann Lesser thought the living room would be a great place. The layout is beautiful and beautifully finished like a fine piece of furniture.

actually leave plenty of room for guests to visit. Of course, most of you aren't going to build layouts in your living rooms. The fact is, we don't usually have much choice as to location; if we're lucky, there's one room and that's it. The job, then, is how to make the room that you do have work. There are basic considerations and some rules we believe are essential to building any successful layout.

RCA

The letters "RCA" identify three rules to follow as you begin to work on your layout: Radius, Clearance, Access. Keep RCA constantly in mind when you're determining where to build the layout and while you're designing the track plan and scenery.

The first rule is to establish the minimum radius curve to which you'll be confined. In other words, how broad must you—or *can* you—make the curves for the equipment you're planning to run? It used to be that on a 4-foot wide table you could turn a train around on 27"- or 31"-radius curves, but today's model locomotives, like a Union Pacific Challenger and scale-length passenger cars, require extra-broad curves. This type of equipment needs at least a 3-foot-radius curve and a 7-foot table width to complete a 180-degree turn. When we designed the JL/ATSF Railway, the longest train equipment we had to consider was 16"-long Lionel light-weight passenger cars.

The next rule is to allow for clearance. Check how much clearance is required on either side of curves and straight track by a locomotive or long car as it overhangs the outer rails and cuts across the inner one. Even small steam locomotives, because of their low-slung side rods, may require greater clearance than you'd expect. As we built the layout we always kept one of those 16"-long lightweight passenger cars close at hand to use as a clearance guide. Sadly, that measurement became inadequate even before we finished the layout. Hi-rail and scale motive power and rolling stock began making their appearance in the hobby stores, but in the space we had available we couldn't redo the track plan to accommodate the wider-radius curves and clearances they required.

Even real railroads have these problems. The Southern Pacific recently completed lowering its mainline track in the tunnels through the famous Tehachapi Pass. Years ago even they couldn't anticipate the greater height of current modular "stack train" containers. With careful planning, and using the largest piece of equipment you plan to run as a clearance guide, your layout will avoid the problem we've had to live with. For now the Cab Forward and E-8 diesels are just nice to look at. Maybe someday we'll build another layout for them to run on.

A final rule in designing a layout is to provide necessary access. Maintenance over all sections of track is critical. Reliable performance of locomotives, rolling stock with sound effects, and electronic remote controls depends on very clean track. Plan also how you're going to get to lower-level tracks or tracks inside a tunnel. Even the best track-cleaning cars can't do *all* the work. And what happens if there's a derailment? You can bet that when you have friends over to see your usually dependable layout, a derailment will occur in the most inaccessible corner! It has something to do with Murphy's Law.

THE TRACK PLAN

How do we want to run our trains? Most of us probably started running them on an oval of track. Then maybe we added a couple of switches, later perhaps a figure eight or dogbone with a reverse loop. How much different will our new Hi-rail layout be? How elaborate do we want it? Is our objective to have lots of trains running at the same time, or do we want "cabs" to control them individually? Do we want trains to prototypically pull out of a freight yard to travel to an endpoint destination and return (i.e., point to point), or do we want them to loop back to their point of origin (point to loop)?

What about that freight yard? Should it include a roundhouse, an engine house, and depending on the era, a turntable? Will there be services for steam locomotives or diesels? All these decisions are fun to consider and must become integral features of a good track plan.

We can learn from fellow modelers in other scales by retaining some kind of track oval in our Hi-rail layouts. Subtly disguised, even in a point-to-point layout design, we thereby allow continuous running whenever we feel like relaxing things a bit or when we have guests in to see the layout.

Clearance is a key in developing your layout. Even though a 16"-long Lionel lightweight passenger car can negotiate this curve, the overhang is most unprototypical. If possible, plan wide curves; if not, don't operate long equipment.

Dilemma here. The 24" turntable bridge isn't long enough for both the hostler engine and the Mikado-type locomotive. Features such as the turntable need to be considered during planning stages. Do you want big locomotives? If so, you'll need a big turntable. Do you have room for only a small turntable? Then you can run only small locomotives. Take time early on and think through the details.

Nothing is more tedious to the non-train enthusiast than watching someone else turn trains and reconfigure them for the next run on a point-to-point layout.

Kalmbach Publishing Co. has several track-planning books in their line; don't feel obligated to build the layouts in the scales specified. Look for inspiration, ideas you can adapt. A useful tool for drawing your own layout track plan is the Layout Design Kit from C.T.T., Inc. This template (for use with three-rail sectional track) and graph paper greatly simplify the job and make track-plan-doodling sessions a lot more productive.

Another essential part of the planning stage is determining how to integrate both operating and static accessories. Where on the JL/ATSF, for instance, were the Lionel bascule bridge, sawmill, icing platform, and milk car platform going to go? Considerations based on RCA, specifically Clearance and Access, helped. If you'll be reloading sawmill logs or cubes of ice, these accessories have to be located close to the front of the layout and on the side of the track where you'll best be able to see their action.

Begin with your largest structures or accessories. Roundhouse and turntable space is determined by the number of engine stalls and by the longest locomotive you intend to turn on the turntable's bridge. A passenger depot requires lengthy loading and unloading platforms. Figure that length into your planning, along with other railside service facilities you'd like in the depot area.

Once you know all the "givens and druthers," as track-planning expert John Armstrong calls them, get out your scale rule, track-planning template, and sharp pencils with new erasers, and start doodling. This, in itself, is an enjoyable part of the hobby. The trick is to fit in all of your "givens and druthers" without making the layout too crowded.

Be sure to keep vertical design in mind also. If your tracks go up, they must do so over a reasonable distance, or else your locomotives won't make the grade.

We were particularly fortunate in having an architect for a friend. With his knowledge and computer equipment, he was able to reproduce our track plan sketches as a scale drawing once we gave him the necessary data, including overall dimensions of the layout, shape, dimensions of various track sections, width of track and ties, and the vertical separation required to cross over the top of the lower track.

The computer printout complete, we took the original to a blueprint company and had copies made inexpensively. We used these extra drawings to plan wiring, scenery, and position of structures and accessories. They came in handy for painting track schematics on the cab control panels. The schematics have also proved invaluable as a reference for electrical troubleshooting. Whether *your* final plans are hand-drawn or computer-generated, we highly recommend having copies made.

Prototype tracks are referred to by name or number. The practice is seldom used on model railroads, yet it is fun to do and a simple way to add realism at no cost. All you need is your track diagram with room to pencil in correct railroad terminology.

MAIN LINE: The single-track part of the railroad (including track that passes through yards) on which trains operate by timetable and signals. In employee timetables, train directions are designated almost exclusively as east and west, regardless of geography.

DOUBLE-TRACK MAIN LINE: On a double-track railroad, trains, with a few exceptions, keep to the right. A train going west on the right-hand track is running on the westward main line, and a train going east on the left-hand track is running on the eastward main line.

Should train movements over these tracks be controlled by Centralized Traffic Control (CTC), a railroad may have both tracks signaled for train movements in either direction, in which case nomenclature changes to "north track" and "south track" where timetable directions are westward and eastward, and "east track" and "west track" where timetable directions are northward and southward.

Some railroads number their main tracks. Usually, the westward main line is "track no. 1" and the eastward main line is "track no. 2," a practice in keeping with using odd numbers for westward trains and even numbers for those going eastward.

MULTIPLE-TRACK MAIN LINE: On some large railroads multiple tracks are assigned to handle only passenger or freight movements in a specific direction, a designation that can easily become complex. Modelers can simplify this situation by remembering that passenger trains must be on a track with a station platform if scheduled for a stop.

SIDINGS OR PASSING TRACKS: A siding is a place where an inferior (lower priority) train can clear (get out of the way of) a superior (higher priority) train. A siding's car capacity and length are listed in the timetable or special instructions, and trains are directed to use the siding by timetable, train order, or signal authority.

Sidings in multiple-mainline territory are further designated as westward or eastward, or they may be given a name the dispatcher will specify to avoid possibility of error or misunderstanding.

INDUSTRIAL TRACKS: Industrial tracks are often named for the business they serve. Should the business have several tracks, a number is usually added to the name. For example, the two tracks in a Purina Chows grainery could be named "Purina 1" and "Purina 2."

YARD TRACKS: Yard tracks are generally designated in two ways. The most common numbers them consecutively, beginning with the track adjacent to the main line as track no. 1. When there are tracks on both sides of the main line, those tracks are designated as north and south (or east and west) yards and use the same consecutive number identification. The track that diverges from the main line into the yard tracks to be used by yard engines to switch those tracks is properly called the "lead track."

SERVICE TRACKS: Tracks surrounding a yard are commonly given names such as caboose, scale house, stock, ice, house (freight) track, etc. Engine-service area tracks may include the names inbound service, wash, outbound ready, ashpit, cinder pit, oil, sand, coal, steam, water plug, diesel fuel, layover, and storage track.

INTERCHANGES AND WYES: Classically speaking, an interchange is where two different railroad main lines cross with a curved track connection between them, the curved connection enabling the routing or "interchange" of cars between the two railroads. A minority of railroads prefer to call this a "transfer track." Where a junction includes connecting tracks that allow a 180-degree end-for-end reversal of cars or locomotives, that junction is called a "wye" and is further identified by its geographic location—for example, "Summit Wye."

Creativity: Armed with the basics, you can now have fun naming and numbering each track segment on your layout. Prototype railroads often use highly descriptive names, and so can you; but most of all, naming tracks will add realism to your railroad.

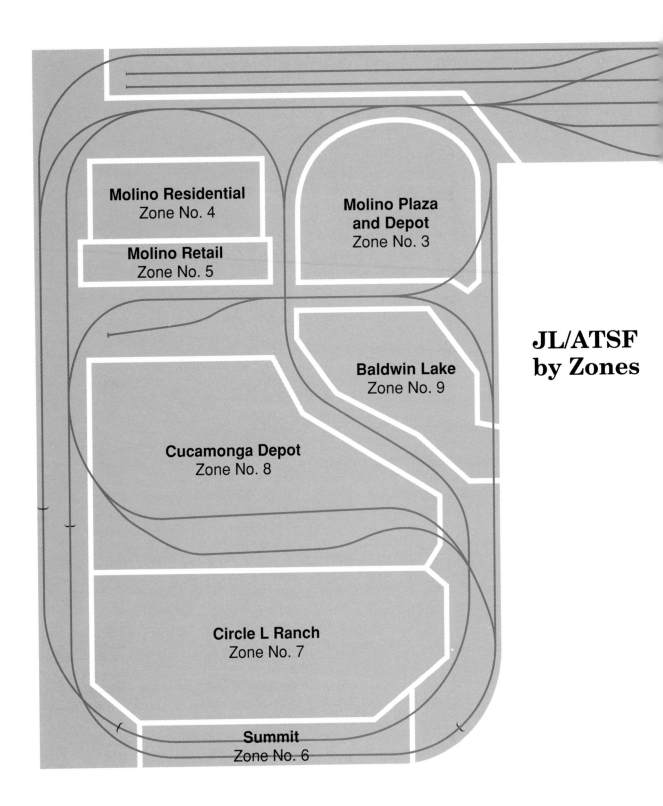

Molino Residential
Zone No. 4

**Molino Plaza
and Depot**
Zone No. 3

Molino Retail
Zone No. 5

Baldwin Lake
Zone No. 9

JL/ATSF
by Zones

Cucamonga Depot
Zone No. 8

Circle L Ranch
Zone No. 7

Summit
Zone No. 6

LAYOUT ZONES

Before you begin to build benchwork, consider your approach to building the layout. Are you going to build all benchwork, lay all track, do all wiring, build all scenery in that order? Or are you going to build your layout in sections? What will determine your approach is the degree of patience you can exercise: how far can you go before you just *have* to run trains?

We took a "zone" approach to building the JL/ATSF, dividing the layout into nine zones (see fig. 2-1).

1. Roundhouse/Turntable
2. Freight Yard

Freight Yard	Roundhouse/
Zone No. 2	Turntable
	Zone No. 1

3. Molino Plaza and Depot
4. Molino Residential
5. Molino Retail
6. Summit
7. Circle L Ranch
8. Cucamonga Depot
9. Baldwin Lake

We completed each zone before proceeding to the next one. This way we always had the feeling of making progress, and visitors and family could see areas of completion rather than vast areas of bare benchwork or unfinished scenery.

To give you an idea of how we worked, we began at the extreme northeast end of the layout with roundhouse and turntable construction. From that point we continued west, building the freight yard along the north wall, a length of 26 feet.

While one of us (Joe) worked on the freight yard's roadbed and electrical wiring, the other (Pete) was building structures and detailing them (even Lionel operating accessories) to look more realistic.

It took us an entire year to finish the freight yard from the time we began the layout benchwork and trackwork. By then we also had complete operating capability. This zone, which occupies the longest stretch of the layout and has plenty of operational activity, gave us the incentive to proceed into the next.

Yard detail items like signposts, crossbucks, junk, etc., came later as we either thought about them, saw them advertised in model railroad magazines, or selected them from research, which included field trips to the prototype.

Note: Lest you think we are incredibly well disciplined, you should know that we temporarily tacked track to the bare plywood, connected wires to a ZW transformer, and were off and running. . . . long before any of the roadbed and intricate wiring to follow was implemented.

There's not a model railroader alive who can wait until the layout is built before running trains. In fact, it's a good idea to keep testing the layout at each step of the process.

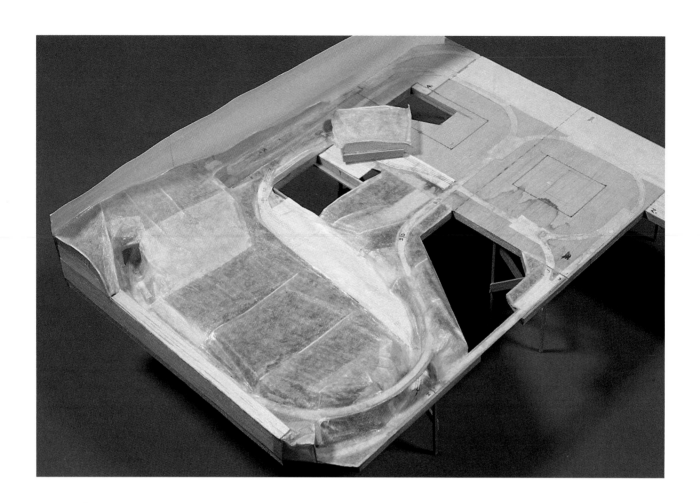

3 Construction

"CREATURE COMFORTS" should be provided for before you begin building your layout. You want to be comfortable while building the layout, as well as later on when you're maintaining and operating it. This involves planning; you need to think about selecting a proper location for the layout, anticipating electrical and lighting needs, allowing space above and beneath the layout, making the layout space attractive and inviting. After all, you're going to spend a lot of time now and in the future with your trains.

Most of us have had to, at one time or another, descend rickety staircases to bare-bulb lighted basements or crawl on hands and knees in low-ceilinged attics to see layouts. Having a layout under those conditions is probably better than having no layout at all, but I'm not sure that building a layout under those conditions is a task suited to the human

A three-dimensional model made of balsa helped the authors to visualize the completed project, plan their benchwork, and anticipate potential problems, including the need for access hatches.

body. Besides, temperatures reaching 120 degrees in the summer and a cool 40 degrees—or less!—in the winter play havoc with modeling materials. If at all possible, consider an alternate space.

Building the JL/ATSF in the house avoided extremes and gave us easy access to the outdoors, where many of the dusty jobs (like sawing wood for the benchwork) could be accomplished. And it was easy to open windows for ventilation when we were using toxic materials such as glues and paints.

Sufficient electrical outlets are also mandatory. Before constructing benchwork, make sure the chosen room has plenty of 110-volt outlets wired and grounded according to local code. Wiring 110 volts is a lot different from the usually harmless 12 to 18 volts required to run trains. (Warning: These connections must be made properly to avoid the possibility of a dangerous, potentially fatal, electrical shock. Those unfamiliar with 110-volt AC wiring should not attempt these projects without consulting a professional electrician.) Try to have outlets wired to more than one circuit breaker. With a medium to large layout it's sometimes easy to overload a single circuit.

Movable work lights above and below the layout during construction are essential. The work you'll be doing requires not just adequate but very good lighting. Clamp-on reflector lamps, which you can purchase in most hardware stores, do a great job. They're easy to move around, and they provide more than adequate illumination. For work above the layout, we used large photo reflectors (with 200-watt bulbs) on stands; for working beneath the layout, we used reflector lamps with 100-watt bulbs. How about carpeting or some kind of soft flooring material under the layout? Although the living room floor was already carpeted before we began work on the layout, we had to resort to knee pads to avoid getting surfer's knees, and believe me, neither of us is an accomplished surfer!

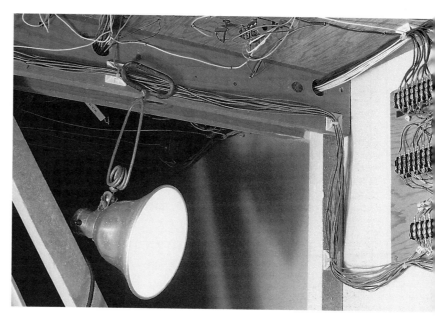

Perhaps nothing made working under the layout so bearable as plenty of light. Clamp-on lights such as this one are inexpensive and provide plenty of illumination.

Another comfort consideration is the height of the layout above the floor. Or from the opposite point of view, the headroom you'll have when working under the layout. Height requirements will vary depending on how tall you are and how elaborate the layout's scenery is—there are some layouts where the river basins or valleys drop all the way to the floor.

Keep in mind that there will be wiring to do below the layout, and you must have sufficient room to work. Consider the usual layout table and open-grid type of benchwork and think about how you'll be working beneath it. Will you sit, kneel, or stand? We found that you need a layout height of at least 43" above the floor to be comfortable while working in a sitting position under the layout on such tasks as pulling wires, soldering connections, or installing switch machines.

In a basement layout this might not be a problem, but you won't find many living rooms without windows. The two windows in the Lesser living room are mostly concealed behind Masonite backdrops painted by Pony Horton.

BENCHWORK

A balsa mock-up model provided an excellent three-dimensional visual-aid for construction of the benchwork. The model indicated in detail where each piece of lumber would go. A copy of a computer printout of the track plan, appropriately scaled and cut to fit the top of the mock-up, helped us determine the location of tracks, hills and valleys, a lake, and even railroad grades. We stretched and doped model airplane silkspan paper across balsa scenery braces to visualize topography. We even located and modeled the access hatches.

A model like this also helps you to visualize the space you'll have when working beneath the layout. It's difficult to anticipate the exact location of all benchwork legs and crossbraces, but try to foresee difficult areas where you'll need access. For example, to clean tracks in a tunnel you have to reach the entire covered section, and poorly placed benchwork braces can really be annoying.

Another annoyance we didn't anticipate was the 1" holes we had to drill through crossbraces after the benchwork was completed. It would have been much better to anticipate where the bundle of electrical wires would penetrate and to have drilled those large holes before installing the wood braces. It's amazing how much sawdust drilling a 1" hole generates, and it's cumbersome at best to vacuum under the table every time you drill a hole.

If your layout plan can't accommodate access hatches for later maintenance, consider in advance specific areas on top of the layout for walking on or sitting. Don't forget access to ceiling lights where bulbs will need replacing from time to time. They must be reached without having to step on a mountain or into a lake. One way to effect this on-the-table access is to design a small section of removable scenery not much larger than where you'll place your feet.

The typical layout room has windows and structural pillars. Location and height of the backdrop will determine whether or not these obstacles must be addressed. Cover windows immediately behind the backdrop permanently (or at least with some type of shade), because the light pouring through an uncovered window and over the top of the backdrop can be distracting and makes viewing the layout difficult. Pillars are more of a problem and may have to be worked into the scenery (e.g., disguised as an oil tank, a smokestack, or hidden inside a high-rise).

On the JL/ATSF Railway, we decided to cover two walls beyond the layout with a scenic backdrop made from sheets of tempered Masonite. It's 30" high and permanently covers parts of two windows.

SCREWS AND NAILS

Good benchwork is the foundation of any layout, and it should be carefully constructed. Many how-to books touch on building benchwork for specific layouts; Linn Westcott's *How to Build Model Railroad Benchwork* (Kalmbach Publishing Co.), details the theories and principles of building benchwork for any model railroad. Nevertheless, no matter how carefully we planned, changes had to be made even after the layout was finished. When you modify the benchwork, try to foresee how you'll cause the least disturbance to fragile details on top of the layout. On most layouts hammering in or pulling out nails causes extreme, often destructive, vibration. An electric drill and wood screws are obviously the smarter choice for benchwork assembly and later modifications—and there *will* be modifications.

Benchwork Construction Tools

The truth is that benchwork can be built entirely with hand tools, but inexpensive power tools make the job a lot easier. Here's what you'll need:

ELECTRIC DRILL: A ⅜" model with reversing and variable speed is ideal. Drill bits will drill pilot holes for screws and a screwdriver bit will drive the screws home. If you have an old electric drill without variable speed, use it to drill pilot holes, and use the variable-speed drill to drive in the screws. Using both in this manner will greatly speed up the construction time.

CROSSCUT HANDSAW: Cutting 1 x 4 girders, joists, braces and risers, 1 x 2 girder flanges, or 2 x 2 legs is easily done with a regular crosscut handsaw. With care, cuts will be as true and square as with a power saw.

ELECTRIC SABER SAW: An electric saber saw is perfect for trimming ends of joists or even sawing through them for benchwork modifications. When cutting subroadbed from plywood, the saber saw is unbeatable, but work patiently and use sharp blades.

SAFETY GLASSES: Always wear them when using power tools. It's all too easy to suffer serious eye damage from fragments of material propelled outward at great velocity by power tools, so remember the old axiom "better safe than sorry."

When cutting plywood, it's also a good idea to wear a dust or paint mask. Resins used in bonding the wood that constitutes plywood can irritate both the skin and the respiratory system. Chances are that when you're cutting subroadbed pieces you'll be at it for some time and stand to breathe a lot of plywood dust and fumes.

C-CLAMPS: The benchwork builder's third hand. Before fastening everything together with screws, C-clamps hold the work so that it can be temporarily positioned and checked. A half dozen with 4" or wider jaws will be most helpful.

SCREWDRIVERS: A pair of good quality slotted and Phillips-head screwdrivers matched to the size screws you're using will be indispensable for those few times when there isn't room for the powered version.

Good benchwork: Like the foundation of a house, benchwork is the base upon which you create your railroad. Build it solid and true, and you'll have a foundation that will ease considerably the construction of problem-free trackwork.

It's called forward
thinking. Even
before the layout
was completed,
the authors knew
that the edge
would be finished
with molding
strips. Even in a
basement or
garage, details like
this make your lay-
out special.

We began building the layout with an older corded electric drill, which had to be constantly plugged into another outlet every time one of us moved to a different location—a real nuisance to say the least. Today, you can buy a good, cordless, multiple-speed electric drill for $30. It's money well spent!

Phillips-head screws and a matching bit assure minimal slippage when driving screws into the wood. The size of screws to be used depends on the thickness of wood to be joined, and having two or three different sizes at hand makes the job a lot easier. Try not to let the drill slip and destroy the screw's slots. If the screw should have to be backed out, the job is a real "bear"! Go slowly, put adequate weight on the drill as you're driving screws, and the bit won't slip.

A mistake we made while constructing benchwork was to use carpenter's glue in addition to screws.

Westcott recommends this; we disagree. It's not really necessary to give benchwork that added strength. The problem occurs when you try to remove a brace that's been glued. Glue is forever, but your benchwork may not be.

When considering how to finish the front of the benchwork, I found that 1 x 4 bracing provided an ample edge to attach decorative molding strips that give the layout a nice finished look. This type of prefinished molding is available from home supply and lumber companies. All we had to do was fasten it with small nails, set the nails, apply wood filler to the nail holes, and touch up the stain to give the molding a fine, finished appearance.

GETTING STARTED

With the living room cleared of furniture, we began building the benchwork outside in the yard, then

Having room to work can make all the difference. Joe and Pete started the actual layout building by moving everything out of the living room.

Framing for the yard was built outside in the (where else?) yard. Wall braces fastened to the plaster wall studs support the long expanse of the freight yard.

installed it, starting with the framing for the 26-foot-long by 30"-wide freight yard. Inside, we attached wall braces to the plaster wall's studs for greater strength. Fastened with 3"-long drywall screws, the braces are more than strong enough to support the plywood tabletop.

All the benchwork, including the cut-out elevated track sections, was set in place at the first construction stage of the layout. We also cut out the three previously designed access hatches. We had thought they would work fine as liftouts. . . . wrong! It proved impossible to lower an entire

ABOVE: Bench-work for the main-line portion of the layout was built in place, in the living room. The window in the background ended up mostly covered by the painted backdrop

RIGHT: Lift-out hatches can work in some situations. In the case of the JL/ATSF, however, hatches hinged to drop down below the layout and fasten upside down (with scenery and structures securely fastened) proved to be a better solution.

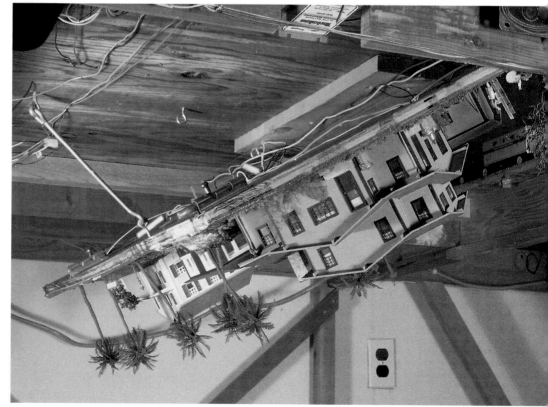

hatch covered with scenery through the opening to place it out of the way on the floor. It was also impractical to have to rely on a second person constantly standing by to take the liftout hatch from the person lifting it. We eventually added hinges to the hatches so they could swing down underneath the layout and hook up out of the way. This approach has worked perfectly.

This retrofit of access hatches reminds me of what John Armstrong said in his book *Creative Layout Design* (Kalmbach Publishing Co.). "If you don't plan things out thoroughly in advance, model railroading is fun! If you do make thoughtful, well-integrated plans for your 'empire,' model railroading can be even more fun."

Make any access to the underside of the layout as easy as possible. It's difficult enough crawling on the floor with your hands full, let alone having to snake over benchwork bracing. After all, this is model railroading, not basic training!

Layout Lighting

The wisest time to think about layout lighting is right after you've decided on a final track plan. Installing the lighting system will be much easier if you do it immediately after the benchwork is finished, or even before then. Types of light and their fixtures make a difference, so here are a few points to consider.

FLUORESCENTS: More efficient than incandescents in converting electricity to light, fluorescents are available in a variety of hues based on the coating applied to the inside of the gas-filled tube. The "color" of light is measured in degrees Kelvin, a system of measurement derived from the light emitted by a "black body" heated to a temperature sufficient to give off light, a process which begins to produce useful visible light at approximately 1000°K. Fluorescent lamps are rated using this color temperature measurement of "chromaticity" and further categorized by descriptive names and a Color Rendering Index (CRI). This can be confusing because CRI can be used only to compare lamps of the same color (Kelvin) temperature. For example, Warm white (CRI 57) and Deluxe warm white (CRI 77) both have a color temperature of 3000°K; Cool white (CRI 62) and Deluxe cool white both have color temperatures of 4150° to 4175°K. Yet if we compare Daylight (6250°K, CRI 75) to Deluxe warm white (3000°K, CRI 77), while the CRIs are almost the same, colors will appear much more realistic under the less harsh Deluxe warm white. As a rule, warm white fluorescents give off light that complements the reddish coloration common to the American southwest, while cool whites complement the hazy blues and greens more common to the rest of the country.

Be aware that all fluorescents can cause color fading and deterioration over time due to their ultraviolet radiation. That means not only scenery, but also trains! The best prevention against the problem is to cover the lamps with filter material or sleeves that block the ultraviolet rays. One supplier is Solar-Screen, 53-11 105th Street, Corona, NY 11368.

INCANDESCENTS: A standard 100-watt incandescent lamp has a color temperature of about 2900° Kelvin. Photo lamps can run up to 3400°K, close to the maximum 3655°K, at which point the tungsten used in the filament melts. By comparison, the sun straight above at noon is rated at approximately 5600°K. (The higher the Kelvin rating, the more the light favors blue in color.) Four 150-watt reflector flood lamps (with built-in reflectors) take 600 watts to operate. Three fluorescent fixtures with two 400-watt lamps in each would total only 240 watts and would give off almost the same amount of light as the incandescent floods.

Summary: Initially fluorescents are more expensive to buy, cost less to operate than incandescents, and are more power-efficient; however, they can cause color fading if not protected by filters. Incandescents, cheaper to install, are more easily and inexpensively dimmed, come in a great variety of color choices, give off much more heat (especially on larger layouts), and cost more to operate. The choice you make should fit your particular situation. Just remember that good layout lighting goes a long way in improving realism.

4 Right-of-Way

REALISTIC RIGHT-OF-WAY, in our opinion, is what distinguishes a Hi-rail layout. It's not difficult to create a good-looking right-of-way, but to do the job right, as with any other endeavor, preparation is critical and you need to spend time looking at the real thing. Also, be aware that a right-of-way varies in appearance throughout the country and on different railroads within the same geographic area.

The quality of the work you do in building your right-of-way will, to a large extent, determine how well your trains run and how good they look as they ride the rails. We can't overemphasize how important it is to exercise extreme care when you build the base for the roadbed (subroadbed), when you lay down the roadbed itself, and when you lay the track. This is the foundation for the object of the layout—running your trains.

Because the right-of-way is also the *focal point* of the layout—you can't miss it if you're watching your trains run—you need to give it careful modeling attention and scenic consideration as well. It needs to look good.

Looking at Track

Take the time to go out and look at real railroad track and you'll discover that it doesn't all look the same. Take the time to model those differences on your layout and your track will become much more realistic.

MAINLINE TRACK: Mainline roadbed is usually raised a foot or two above the surrounding right-of-way terrain in a variety of grade profiles. Generally the ballast is clean and its crown (the highest point) is close to the top of the center of the ties. Duplicating this exact profile in model form is both difficult and unnecessary, but laying the track on cork roadbed with beveled edges raises it acceptably and allows for ballast to be glued between the ties, parallel to them on the outside of the rails, and to the beveled edge slopes. Two or more side-by-side mainline tracks can have the ballast line level all the way across, which is prototypical.

SIDING AND PASSING TRACK: Where a single mainline track serves traffic from both directions, the siding or passing track is usually somewhat lower. The ballast line isn't quite as straight and well-maintained, the ballast color is somewhat darker, its beveled edge slopes are shallower, and if the track is used infrequently, weeds and grass grow up through it. Don't forget to blend the ballasts gradually where the siding or passing track closes with the mainline track.

INDUSTRIAL TRACK: Usually set below the main line, as with sidings and passing tracks, industrial track also uses a slight upward gradient to rejoin the main. Lacking a well-defined profile, tie tops are often level with the surrounding right-of-way terrain and ballast barely visible where weeds and grass proliferate. An exception is when a new industrial track is built. There, for a while, the track will have good ballast edges comparable to those of the main line.

YARD TRACK: Again, yard track is set lower than the main line on right-of-way as flat as the surrounding terrain. New yard track can have clean ballast, but it will still be flat. Old yard track will have dirty ballast that is almost undiscernible. Model yard track ballast should, therefore, be finer and of a darker shade than any other ballast on your layout. Further realism can be achieved if you mix in some fine dirt and let everything spill over the tops of the ties (which should also be darker) at random.

SWITCHES: With model switches, avoid getting any ballast between the "header" ties (the two long ones that guide the switch throwbar). This precaution will prevent ballast particles from fouling the movement of the switch points and operating linkage.

Santa Fe Ry. photograph

Fig. 4-1. A 2" "Tuf-Grind" wheel cuts through one rail and across to the next.

The visual elements of prototypical mainline right-of-way are:
1. General appearance of the track
2. Height of track above the surrounding level of terrain
3. Ballast and shoulders
4. Rail color.

While it's true that you can see lousy, poorly maintained roadbed on a real railroad, there's no excuse for ours looking that way unless, of course, we choose to duplicate a prototypical section where it really looks like that.

TRACK

Face it—sectional, three-rail, O gauge track is unrealistic. You can, of course, do some things to make it look better. For starters, you can add individual ties between the metal ones to make the track look more believable. A company called Moondog Express manufactures rubber ties that are easy to work with and reasonably inexpensive. Adding only three of their ties between the metal ties of O-31 sections greatly improves the appearance of tinplate track. Painting the sides of the rails (not the running surface) also helps the appearance of Lionel or K-Line track.

On the JL/ATSF, we chose GarGraves' "Phantom" three-rail track. The rails are rust resistant and the center rail is blackened to help disguise its unprototypical presence. GarGraves track also comes with wooden ties, which are realistic and helpful when it comes to wiring the layout. More about this feature later.

It's very important to join all track with great care. Not only is this paramount for good electrical continuity and reduced derailments, but it also looks better. To make track joints tight and clean takes patience, particularly when cutting GarGraves' track after bending a curve. Sectional track has traditionally been cut with a hack saw or side-cutters; we don't recommend either tool.

To cut track, use an electric motor tool fitted with a 2" "Tuf-Grind" cutting wheel (fig. 4-1). The 2" diameter of the cutting wheel allows you to cut through one of the rails and across to the next rail. This guarantees a straight cut across all three rails. The cutting wheel cuts easily through metal, and you can use the side of the wheel to smooth the ends of the rail cuts. Always be sure to wear safety glasses when cutting track. Sparks and bits of metal will fly like crazy, and on occasion the cutting disk itself breaks, sending bits of abrasive shards in all directions.

The same technique and tool can be used when cutting gaps in GarGraves rails for the purpose of breaking electrical continuity (for isolating blocks or activating accessories and signals). For cosmetic purposes, and to keep gaps from closing up due to rail expansion, simply fill the gap with a bit of styrene and two-part 5-minute epoxy. When the epoxy has set hard, file it flush with the rail and dab on a little paint to make it invisible. (Be sure to clearly indicate all gaps on your track plan schematic so you can easily locate them when there's troubleshooting to be done.) Make each gap wide enough so that it can't close and negate the purpose for cutting it in the first place.

Subroadbed and Roadbed

SUBROADBED

On model train layouts, subroadbed is the part of the benchwork construction onto which roadbed and then track is to be fastened. Most modelers prefer to build subroaded in one or more of the following ways.

RIBBON SUBROADBED: Commonly using ½" plywood (some builders prefer ¾", which is heavy to work with), straight and curved sections are first drawn full-size on the sheet material, then cut out with a saber saw before being fitted and fastened to the benchwork like pieces of a puzzle. The process of laying out multiple identical pieces (curves, switch blocks) can be made faster by using the first piece cut as a pattern for the others.

COOKIE-CUTTER SUBROADBED: Best for smaller "flattop" layouts, or yard areas on bigger ones, cookie-cutter subroadbed differs from ribbon subroaded only in that the outlines drawn on the sheet are cut by the saber saw with the material already in place. With the outline cuts made, this part of the sheet can be propped up with temporary risers and clamps to help determine grades and vertical clearances where one track is to cross over another. When everything is satisfactory, risers and subroadbed are fastened permanently.

SPLINE SUBROADBED: Used for years in various ways, spline roadbed is made from long strips of ¼" x 1" soft wood (i.e., white pine, sugar pine, redwood, etc.) glued and clamped on edge to risers. Beginning with the center strip, others are laminated to either side of it until the laminates equal the width desired. Although more time-consuming in construction, spline roadbed encourages graceful flowing curves, easements, and transitions to straight sections.

ROADBED

On top of the subroadbed goes the roadbed (sometimes also referred to as "ballast strip" or "ballast board") onto which track is fastened. Among the most popular roadbed materials are:

CORK ROADBED: Manufactured in 3-foot-long sections split lengthwise into two pieces with outside beveled edges representing sloped ballast shoulders. The cork is simply nailed or glued to the subroadbed where its flexibility, ease in cutting and trimming, and sound-absorbing quality all contribute to its popularity in all scales.

RUBBER ROADBED: Two kinds are currently available. One is molded to mate with individual straight and curved sections of O and O-27 track, the other, made of uncured butyl rubber, comes in self-adhesive rolls of a consistency similar to thick tar. Once rolled out onto the subroadbed, track is pressed into the tacky viscosity of the rubber which locks it in place.

HOMASOTE ROADBED: Homasote is a light gray pressed paper product that comes in ½" thick 4 x 8-foot sheets which can be purchased in many lumberyards. Dense enough to hold spikes or track nails, it has, like cork, excellent sound-absorbing qualities. Its greatest disadvantage is the amount of pervasive dust it generates when cut with a saber saw, and its lack of dimensional stability in climates with high humidity and temperature changes.

MILLED ROADBED: Sometimes commercially available in O scale, milled roadbed is made of high-quality soft wood precut to a variety of curved radii, and straight and switch block pieces, all with beveled outer edges.

For a more comprehensive discourse on subroadbed and roadbed, refer to *How To Build Model Railroad Benchwork* by Linn H. Wescott (Kalmbach Publishing, no. 12041).

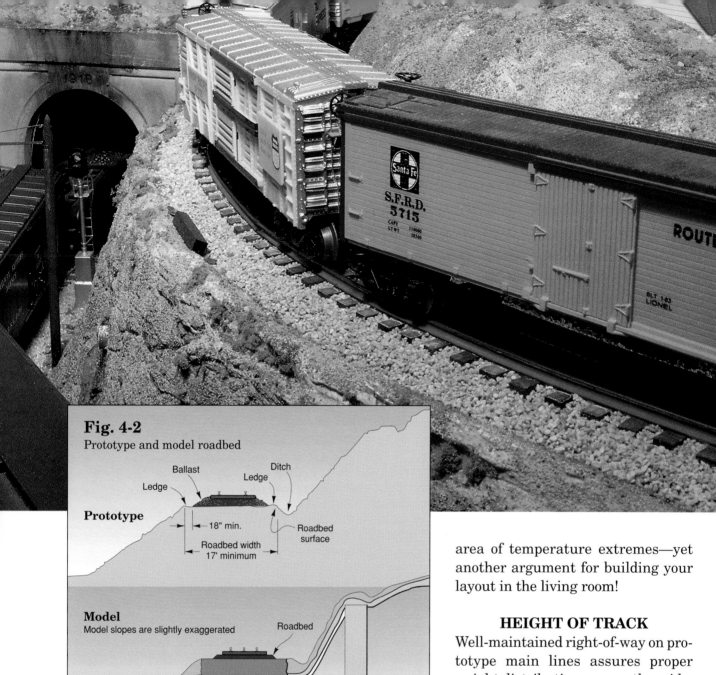

Fig. 4-2
Prototype and model roadbed

Prototype

Ledge
Ballast
Ledge
Ditch
18" min.
Roadbed width 17' minimum
Roadbed surface

Model
Model slopes are slightly exaggerated
Roadbed
Subroadbed

Fig. 4-3 (photo). Mainline roadbed profile is particularly evident alongside Summit Grade.

On the JL/ATSF, we soldered all rail joints to give better electrical continuity and improved performance, then carefully filed away any excess solder that could cause a derailment. Expansion and contraction of the rails (causing buckling or gaps) has long been a subject of debate when it comes to soldering rails. It may be a consideration if your layout is located in an area of temperature extremes—yet another argument for building your layout in the living room!

HEIGHT OF TRACK

Well-maintained right-of-way on prototype main lines assures proper weight distribution, a smoother ride, and good drainage. Track is kept above known high-rainfall levels, but even the best roadbed can't avoid the scourge of flooding as occasionally evidenced in some parts of the United States. Consider too, that melting snow seeps through ballast to settle at a lower level than the rails. If we look at a cross-section of mainline roadbed, a definite profile is apparent (fig. 4-2). While it may be difficult for us to precisely model the height of track above the surrounding layout terrain, by using a variety of roadbed materials, we *can* effectively

Fig. 4-4 (FAR LEFT). Apply the ballast between the rails and along the outside, letting it roll down the beveled edges of the cork roadbed.

Fig. 4-5 (LEFT). Use your forefinger to spread the ballast, lightly pushing it along until even with the tops of the ties.

simulate the profile of the prototype (fig. 4-3).

Currently available is rubber, cork, and vinyl roadbed. On the JL/ATSF we used cork. The thickness of the cork strips gives sufficient elevation to both track and ballast. It's easy to use and quickly adheres to wood with carpenter's glue. When bending the cork on curves, use push pins to hold it in place until the glue dries. After a few hours it's permanently bonded to the plywood. The cork is easy to fit and cut under track switches, and a pass at it with a sharp hobby knife will re-bevel edges to match the other pieces.

In prototype freight yards, track is pretty much at the level of surrounding terrain. We found that ¼"-thick cork sheets worked well to cover the entire length and width of the yard. The cork not only reduced the level of track noise somewhat, but it provided a surface to which scenic material would adhere.

BALLAST

On real railroads, ballast serves a number of purposes. It holds the ties in place, promotes drainage, prevents lateral rail deflection, and helps absorb the weight of passing trains. Its only purpose on a Hi-rail layout is to look pretty. When carefully done, it adds a truly striking effect.

Not surprisingly, the scale of the ballast you select is important. Obviously, you don't want boulders for ballast, and pebbles aren't too convincing either. Ballast is available from several manufacturers. Highball Products offers a wide selection both in size, color, and type. They sell O scale ballast in cinder, dark gray, limestone, iron ore, light gray, and black (coal) in one-pound bags.

Mainline ballast should be spread to the tops of the ties and down the cork roadbed's beveled edges, which simulate its sloped shoulders (fig. 4-4). At the base of the shoulders, the ballast should end in relatively even lines; it shouldn't look like Kitty Litter scattered all around. Extra care taken to make sure there isn't any ballast left on top of the ties will also greatly improve overall realism.

APPLY AND BOND BALLAST

The convenient 16-ounce size of a Highball Products bag of ballast makes it easy to dispense the right amount onto the track. Cut off only a small corner of the bag for pouring. Too much ballast dumped onto the tracks takes more time and effort to spread, so begin by slowly pouring small amounts of ballast between the rails. Use your forefinger to spread it out to the tops of the ties (fig. 4-5). Any

Fig. 4-6 and 4-7 (ABOVE and ABOVE RIGHT). Mist water liberally over the ballast to assure that the glue, applied next, will spread evenly and thoroughly among the ballast pieces. Apply acrylic matte medium (diluted 1 part matte medium to 5 parts water) with a basting syringe.

Fig. 4-8. Note the polished surface of the rails, the darker unpolished sides, and the general look and shading of this stretch of prototype mainline track.

excess can be pushed to the next section of track. Pour more ballast over the ends of the ties, but this time pile it up above the ties, because as you smooth it out, the excess will spill over the side of the beveled cork to form a nearly perfect, natural looking shoulder. Use a small paintbrush to sweep excess ballast off the ties and along to the next section.

Once the ballast is in place, liberally spray the ballast with water mixed with a few drops of liquid dish washing detergent (fig. 4-6). You want the water to be thoroughly absorbed by the ballast so that when glue is applied, it will bond the ballast evenly and thoroughly. The liquid detergent helps the water seep through the

layers of ballast and prevents the glue from balling into droplets. A paper towel can be used to carefully wipe excess water off the rails, but take care that the towel doesn't accidentally drag along on the freshly laid ballast and disturb its uniform, well-maintained appearance.

To bond the ballast, I use matte medium, a Liquitex acrylic available at most art stores. Mix 1 part matte medium with 5 parts water. With a large basting syringe, slowly squeeze the mixture over the top of the ballast (fig. 4-7). Don't be afraid of getting too much on the ballast; it will be absorbed and dry perfectly clear, and any spills onto the ties are okay—it's just another kind of natural weathering.

Fig. 4-9. Paint the inside and outside of the rails Floquil Rail Brown for a rusted effect.

Fig. 4-10. Dab on glossy black paint in spots to simulate freshly dropped oil.

Tunnel Portals

Prototypically speaking, raw railroad economics mandate the smallest possible bore wherever tunneling is unavoidable. As a rule, 50 percent more removal of material realizes only a 25 percent increase in clearance, a negative equation sufficient to encourage many an Eastern coal-hauling railroad of the past to tailor its motive power accordingly. Learning from the prototype, therefore, take into consideration the type of equipment you'll be running before you start building your tunnels and portals and whether any of them will be located on curves where big locomotives and long cars require far greater clearances than smaller, shorter ones.

Tunnel portals are constructed from four basic types of material, reflecting structural need, economics, and geographic location. They are:

MASONRY PORTAL: Masonry blocks measuring about 5 feet by 2 feet are stacked brick-like in overlapping courses to an approximate height of 30 feet and width of 32 feet for single-track tunnel openings. The stonework lining the arched entrance is called a "quoin," common in construction where walls or surfaces meet at angles in an architectural style popularized primarily in the Eastern states from 1890 to 1930.

STONE PORTAL: Complex in appearance, the stone portal is directly related to the masonry portal in construction technique, the major difference being the use of somewhat smaller and more irregular blocks. The quoin configuration around the tunnel mouth is also varied and often is crowned by a raised keystone commonly found decorating Eastern portals.

CONCRETE PORTAL: Poured, reinforced concrete portals can be seen in all parts of the country and are the easiest portals to model. Essentially constructed of horizontal layers of concrete poured into forms containing steel reinforcing rods, the layered joints are easily simulated with scored lines on soft wood topped by an overlay of cardstock or balsa cut out to match the prototype, then also scored prior to painting. Adding to the top of the entrance arch a "concrete" rectangle with black press-on letters showing the year of construction adds

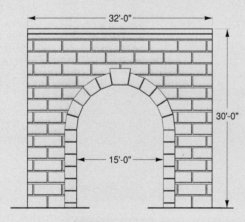

Masonry portal

Stone portal

THE COLOR OF RAILS

Prototype rails aren't a shiny bright tinplate color. Rails—made of steel—rust almost immediately after they are exposed to the elements. Only the tops of mainline rails remain polished because of train wheels continuously running over them (fig. 4-8). But did you ever notice how rusty rails are on an industrial siding that doesn't get much use, or on an abandoned rail line? To model this discoloration, use a good quality 00-size brush and Floquil Rail Brown paint to color the *sides* of the rails (fig. 4-9). Paint only rails that are visible from any viewing angle. There's no reason to paint rails if they can't be seen.

At the same time as you paint the rails, add to the realism by dropping a coat of "oil" on either side of the center rail. All of the muck dropping from locomotives leaves a dirty, oily trail on the ballast. Forget for a moment that history to your layout. Follow this with a light dusting of dry graphite powder feathered at its edges with a soft brush, and the concrete portal will reflect the deposit of steam soot and diesel exhaust gases over the years.

WOODEN PORTAL: Of an earlier vintage when equipment was smaller and clearances tighter, wooden tunnel portals are made from timbers squared roughly to 8½" x 8½", then cut to length and stacked horizontally to be retained by framing and shoring. Due to the straightness of the timbers, the tunnel entrance is angular at the top of the mouth rather than arched. Most often associated with backwoods lumber and mining railroads where construction material is plentiful, the Southern Pacific Railroad's wooden snow sheds through California's Donner Pass were built following a similar technique.

WING WALLS: The topography of the immediate area where the tunnel portal is located determines the need for wing or retaining walls. Their purpose is to keep the surrounding terrain from sliding onto the track. The length, height, and configuration is also determined by the surrounding terrain. Railroads usually use the same material for the wing walls. For masonry or stone portals, wing walls are configured to end in full stones and matching mortar lines at the portal joint. With wooden portals, wing walls are either a continuation of horizontal timbers stacked to be held in place by vertical ones or timbers driven horizontally into the terrain, their protruding ends "cribbed" together by cross timbers.

WITH YOUR tunnel portal in place, prototypical details such as fallen rock tallus at its base, vines clinging to its face, discoloration, a telephone shack, a warning telltale, or even a signal nearby will add credibility and reality to the scene.

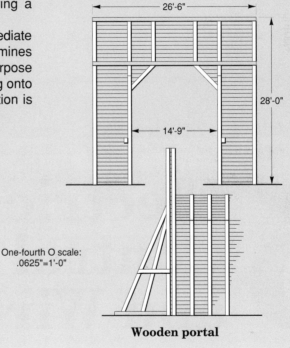

One-fourth O scale:
.0625"=1'-0"

Concrete portal

Wooden portal

the center rail exists and give the entire width between the outside rails a grimy film of black goop . Use an eye dropper filled with a diluted solution of Floquil Grimy Black and Floquil Dio-Sol (1 part paint, 3 parts thinner). The ballast quickly absorbs this mix and leaves a dirty coating that looks very convincing. Dab on a few globs of Testor's Glossy Black paint here and there along the track to simulate newer oil stains that haven't yet soaked into the ground (fig. 4-10).

We completed roadbed construction for the entire JL/ATSF at one time, rather than as a part of a zone described in Chapter 2. Once the process of applying and bonding ballast began, it was much easier to take this task to completion. Details along the right-of-way were completed later, and we'll describe how that's done in Chapter 8, "Details Along the Right-of-Way."

5 Electrical Control and Wiring

The fireman operates the power blocks, switches, and signals from the freight yard control panel while the engineer uses the throttle to regulate the speed of a switcher.

WHEN JOSHUA LIONEL COWEN designed toy trains to run on three-rail track and alternating current (AC), he made electrical control and wiring as simple as it comes. Three-rail track and AC current doesn't involve such complexities as having to reverse track polarity (the flow of electrical current) in order to run locomotives in reverse; nor does it involve reverse loops, as does the two-rail DC wiring used with most scale model railroads.

Regardless of the electrical principles involved, it's ultimately the design and implementation of a well-thought-out electrical control system that makes our trains move realistically—an important consideration for the Hi-railer!

Basic electrical rules for operating three-rail O gauge trains are clearly explained in Roland LaVoie's excellent book, *Model Railroading with Lionel Trains* (Greenberg Publishing, 1989). These rules apply whatever the sophistication of the electrical system. To quote Linn H. Westcott, a pioneer in our hobby, "When you actually do the work, all the mystery will quickly disappear, and soon you may even be giving the other fellow some help."

You can run a railroad in many different ways. We've seen layouts where the operator likes to run his train just as fast as possible, bragging about how it never derails. Another friend enjoys seeing five trains running at a time. . . . round and round, automated signals and all kinds of accessory attractions going wild.

As we planned the wiring and control for the JL/ATSF Railway, our chief goal was to run each locomotive independently, over the same routes, using one transformer per train. Of course, if a layout has totally independent routes of track, each route can have its own transformer and each train can run virtually unattended. It's also possible to automate a complex layout so that there need be very little hands-on operation, but that isn't our idea of realistic operation. Our objective was to totally involve two operators per train—an engineer and fireman. Working together, they plan their train route's electrical blocks and switch alignments, and their only concern is with the train they're running.

When a second and third train runs along the same route, either ahead of or behind the first train, the first train's operators must pay particular attention to turn on and off (electrically) all blocks entered or exited so that a following train can move into them independently. Additionally, the operators are responsible for checking and throwing track switches and activating grade-crossing signals. When guests run trains, we let them use the throttle to regulate the speed of the train while we turn on blocks and align switches.

TRANSFORMERS AND AUXILIARY POWER

There are many transformers from which to choose. When we began to build the layout, we chose the MRC Tech II Trainpower O-27 transformer because we wanted a transformer with a single throttle. We also wanted the throttle to be some kind of handle, giving a more realistic feel than a knob. The Lionel ZW transformer is the traditional first choice, but its two throttle handles are only 10" apart, which doesn't provide much working room for two operators. It might be okay if the operators are respectively left- and right-handed, but they'd still practically be on top of one another, so we ruled out the ZW for running trains. We did use a ZW, however, to satisfy separate auxiliary power requirements for switches, lights, operating accessories, and signals.

For a few years the MRC transformers were adequate, but as more and more power was required for electronic sound systems, lights in passenger cars, and multiple locomotive motors, we had to make a change. During discussion of the problem with several train friends, someone suggested that we try the old Lionel LW transformer. Its power output is rated at 7 amps, while the MRC transformer is rated at only 3 amps. The LW has a single throttle with red buttons for direction and whistle control. With a little hunting around at train meets, we quickly came up with three LWs at an average price of $60. . . . and what a difference! Now we have more than enough power for anything we run on the layout.

ROUTES ALONG THE JL/ATSF

In the preliminary planning stage of a layout, determine how you'd like to electrically separate blocks (sections) of track for the purpose of operating different train routes. A practical and realistic consideration necessitated dividing the layout into two sections: the freight yard and the mainline routes. Operating only from the mainline cab and control panel made it virtually impossible to see trains running at the far end of the freight yard some 36 feet away, so the solution was to build a separate cab and control panel to operate all the train movements in the freight yard.

These cab throttles and their control panel are mounted on a roll-away console that can be stored under the layout. Rolled out, the console is located where it controls operations close at hand. The freight yard includes a roundhouse and turntable, a classification yard, and a pair of

The freight yard console is on casters so that it can be easily rolled out from underneath the yard during operating sessions.

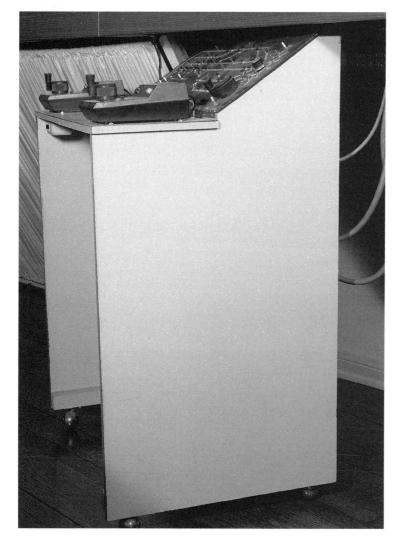

make-up tracks, all wired for independent operation of two locomotives. Here, two MRC O-27 transformers are still more than adequate to power the tracks within the freight yard.

The overall mainline section is approximately 10 x 15 feet and includes three distinct routes. On the schematic (fig. 5-1), we named these routes "River Route 1 and 2" and the "Mountain Route." The River Routes are wired and blocked to run two trains simultaneously, while the Mountain Route is wired to run only one. The mainline cab panel contains all the controls to run these three routes independent of the freight yard.

For added realism and practical operation, the freight yard's two outer tracks are referred to as numbers 1 and 5. They are dedicated to inbound and outbound trains and may be operated by either mainline or freight yard cabs. As such they are the only tracks in the freight yard that can be used by the mainline cab. All other operations within the freight yard are electrically locked out from mainline control. The freight yard cab and control panel are used to classify cars, make up or break apart a train, shuttle cars around for storage, or move locomotives in or out of the roundhouse. "Yard limit" signs inform operators that they are either approaching or leaving the yard. Within the yard they must follow the rules of the yardmaster and turn over control from the mainline cab to the freight yard cab.

BLOCKS

A "block," sometimes called a "control block," is an electrically insulated stretch of track created by cutting a gap in the center rail at the block's boundaries. Electrically powering that rail is accomplished either manually via a toggle switch or automatically with a relay. The length of a

Wire

When you're installing track feeders, use heavier (larger) wire on long runs than on short runs, or the trains will slow down due to resistance. The size of wire is further determined by the amount of current the train requires. For example, if you have very long runs with some sound-equipped locomotives pulling a string of lighted passenger cars, you'll need heavier wire than that needed by a yard switcher shunting individual cars close to the track power supply.

WIRE SIZE: Wire is measured according to the area of the wire's cross section by a unit of measurement called the "circular mil" (for those interested, an area of a circle 0.001" in diameter), and wire comes in AWG (American Wire Gage) sizes. For the sake of comparison, house electrical wiring is normally nos. 12 to 14 AWG wire, and your telephone is wired with no. 24 AWG. The higher the AWG number, the smaller the diameter of the wire.

Generally, sizes run from large wire at no. 0000 AWG to the smallest at no. 40 AWG. For most home Hi-rail layout track-feeder applications, nos. 14 to 16 AWG wire will provide ample current flow. Twin-coil switch machines require many amps to operate properly and should be wired with no. 18 AWG. Interior model building lamps, and street and signal lights will require only nos. 20 to 24 AWG wire.

STRANDED AND SOLID: Wire comes either as stranded or solid. Stranded wire is made by wrapping many single strands together; solid wire is made from only a single strand.

Good locations for stranded wire are anywhere the wire must flex (i.e., power supply cord, hand-held throttle cord, wire running between cars); good locations for solid wire are where the wire won't flex (i.e., under the layout). Although many combinations of numbers of individual strands can be used to make a particular size of stranded wire, its AWG number will always coincide precisely with the same AWG number for solid wire.

INSULATION: Insulation is normally rated for the maximum voltage that can safely be used in a wire. Because we seldom use more than 24 volts in our model train applications, we are well below the maximum ratings of the wire's insulation.

Color-coding of wire insulation is most helpful when tracing a wire from its point of origin to its destination, and it's a time-saving investment to buy wire in various colors to permit dedication of a certain color to a certain purpose. Imagine trying to solve a future wiring problem if the color of the wire's insulation changes several times between two points!

WIRE TOOLS: Working with wire requires some simple tools. You should have an inexpensive adjustable stripper/cutter for cutting wire and stripping its insulation, and you'll want two pairs of small pliers: one diagonal-cutting and one long-nose. Both are very useful overall.

More information: If you're interested in learning more about wire and wiring, an excellent book is *Basic Electricity and Electronics for Model Railroaders* by Don Fiehman (Kalmbach Books no. 12083). Also helpful are Peter Riddle's books on wiring, specifically pertaining to three-rail wiring: Greenberg's *Wiring Your Lionel Layout, Volume 1: A Primer for Lionel Train Enthusiasts* (Greenberg no. 10-7555) and Greenberg's *Wiring Your Lionel Layout, Volume 2: Intermediate Techniques* (Greenberg no. 10-7560).

block is determined by the length of the longest train that will occupy it.

There are 20 blocks in the JL/ATSF freight yard alone. Some blocks are only the length of a locomotive (the tracks in the roundhouse, for example), while blocks on tracks 1 and 5 are long enough to handle an entire train.

Because some trackage along the main line is common to both River and Mountain Routes, 18 blocks had to be laid out to manage this added complexity. While in theory each block should be long enough for the longest train, it may be necessary to add very short blocks to some areas of your layout where two routes use common tracks. On the JL/ATSF's 90-degree crossover track, which is used by both routes, the block extends only 10" in each direction. It has to be turned on or off quickly when the locomotive

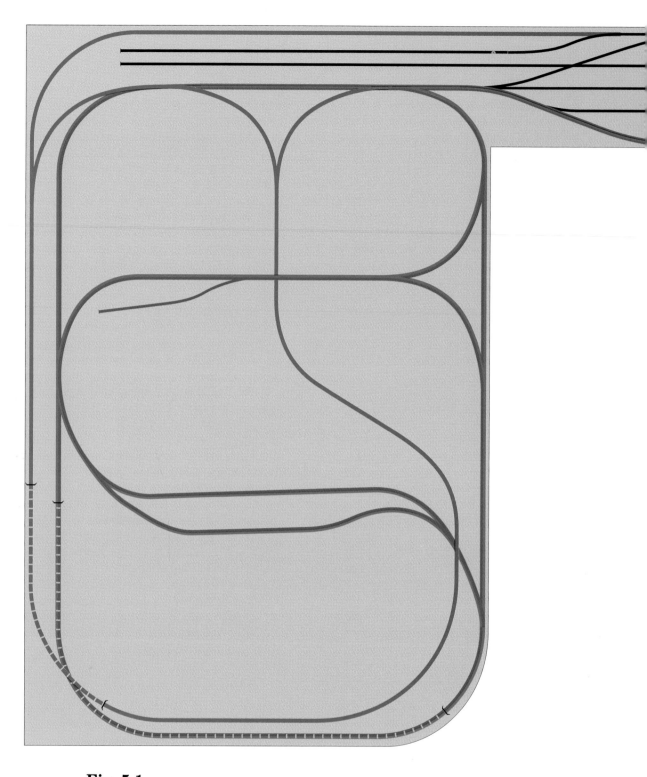

Fig. 5-1
JL/ATSF Traffic Routes

▬▬ Mountain Route
▬▬ River Route No. 1
▬▬ River Route No. 2

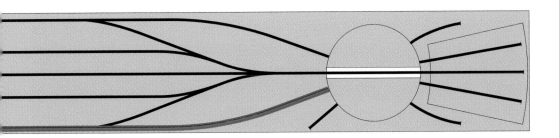

The mainline cab panel consists of three Lionel LW transformers and controls for power blocks, track switches, signals, and lights. Mounted on the wall behind Pete, Joe, and Jo Ann is the mainline CTC panel. Visitors love to watch the lights move around the board almost as much as they enjoy watching the trains themselves! William Garnet photo

passes over it to keep from interfering with the power of the other routes.

WIRING AND OPERATING A BLOCK

A block is easy to wire and operate. For each block, a double pole, double throw (DPDT) center-off toggle switch is wired between the transformer and the track. We use Radio Shack mini DPDT toggle switches (cat. no. 275-620). These toggles move either left or right to electrically connect the block to the corresponding left or right throttle. The toggles are "off" in the center position so that the block can be made electrically dead. The operator is responsible for returning the toggle's bat handle back to the center-off position after his or her train leaves the block.

Each DPDT toggle has six posts. Feeder wires for track power are connected to the center posts. Only the

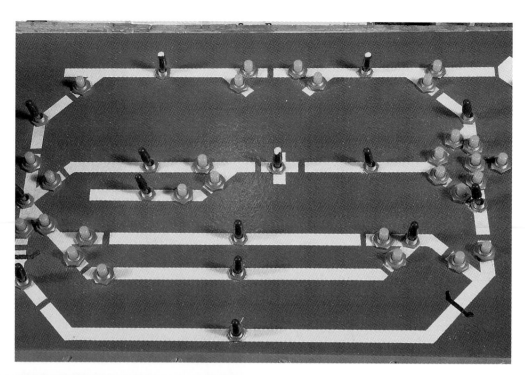

RIGHT: Gaps in the track schematic indicate individual power blocks. Any toggle switch with a white tip indicates a power block shared by two cabs. It's the operators' responsibility to center the toggles when they leave a block.

BELOW: The 90-degree crossover track is used by both routes. It has its own power block extending only 10" in each direction.

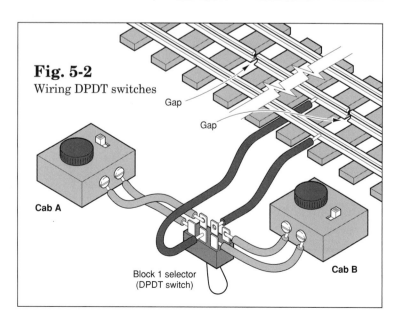

Fig. 5-2
Wiring DPDT switches

Gap

Gap

Cab A

Block 1 selector
(DPDT switch)

Cab B

wire leading to a particular block's center rail need be connected directly to the track. The outside ("common") rail power wire can be connected in series looped from one toggle to the next and then to the outside rail. See fig. 5-2. After experimenting with different sizes of wire (or "gages," as wire is usually coded), we recommend no less than 16 gage wire for track power. For series connections between toggle switches in the console, we suggest 18 gage wire, but from the last toggle in the series to the track, we again used 16 gage wire. Multistrand, rather than solid copper, wire is easier to work with because it's flexible, easy to thread into tight spots, and easy to solder.

We chose wire with red insulation to identify center rail power and white for outside rail power. For troubleshooting purposes it's a good idea to be consistent in your selection of wire. Choose colors that are easily identified, such as black, white, yellow, and bright red. This will be very helpful when you're trying to trace a specific wire in a bundle and the nearest

Each of these wires (color-coded also) indicates a different power source. The numbered flags coincide with a master wiring identification list for easy recognition.

identifying number is many feet away.

For those of you who are color-blind, it's paramount that you further identify all wires by attaching an identifying label to both ends of a connection and record the numbers on a corresponding schematic. To number wires, apply a short strip of masking tape to a flat surface (glass is ideal), write the desired number on each with a Sharpie extra-fine-point permanent marker, then carefully lift the tape off the surface. Snip each pair of numbers and fold them flag-like over each end of the wire lead.

Run all wires originating from track, switches, lights, and accessories to terminal strips (attached to the underside of the benchwork) and attach them with spade lugs. On the JL/ATSF, wires never run more than 5 feet from the terminal strips to the cabs, so there we used multi-conductor cables with as many as fifty 18-gage wires per cable. We calculate the length we need to run the cable from the terminal strip to the farthest end of the control panel, then add another couple of feet to compensate for any miscalculation. Then we cut the cable, peel away the outside sheath, and enlisting the aid of Jo Ann Lesser, attach a number to each end of the cabled wire. (Jo Ann's help was important in keeping Joe, who is color-blind, from making color or continuity mistakes when attaching the wires to toggle or transformer posts.)

TRACK SWITCHES

Railroad companies always keep their switches set to mainline (normal) routes for safety and speed. Siding and spur switches are often manually set by a fireman or brakeman. Today, most switches are operated by remote control from a Central Traffic Control center where sophisticated sensors monitor safe operation. The JL/ATSF Railway trains share mainline tracks, and their operators can't always be sure that switches are properly aligned for an approaching train. Furthermore, track schematics are too crowded at the cab panels for red and green switch position indicator lights, so the rule is to electrically

Each under-the-table switch machine installation has an NJ International twin solenoid and an Eshleman linkage.

Walthers two-light dwarf signals are used in the freight yard to regulate train movements.

throw each switch beforehand, regardless of whether it's thought to be aligned or not.

When we began constructing the layout, we had a choice of Lionel's two types of right- and left-hand switches, GarGraves switches, or Right-Of-Way Industries switches. For the first time in O gauge three-rail, Right-Of-Way offered a comprehensive selection of switches. The ability to design the

layout knowing we could purchase three-way switches, curved switches, wyes, double-slips, either O-72 or regular, enabled us to achieve a degree of realism far greater than previously possible. The layout, as it turned out, uses 31 Right-Of-Way switches.

Unlike Lionel switches, Right-Of-Way switches don't come with electrical solenoids to operate them. The user must not only install a switch

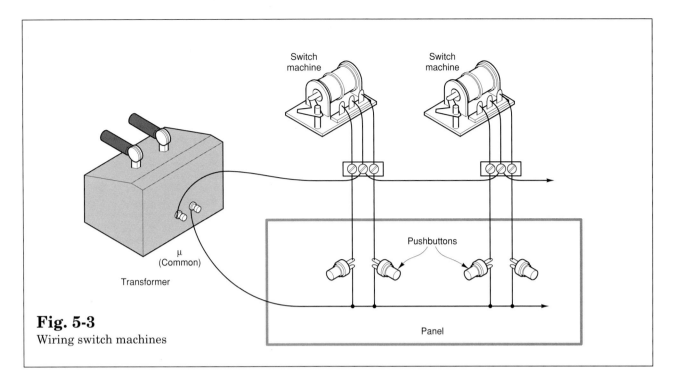

Fig. 5-3
Wiring switch machines

machine but devise a control to activate it. Fortunately, such mechanisms have been used in other scales for many years, and so it became a matter of adapting the best known system to the layout. Probably the most universally used switch machine is the twin-solenoid type manufactured over the years by companies like Tenshodo, Kemtron, and NJ International. They are virtually identical in design and relatively inexpensive. For duplicating the slower, prototypical movement of switch points, slow-motion machines like the "Switchmaster" or "Tortoise" are tops. Another innovative switch control system, designed and manufactured by Del-Aire Products, is pneumatic. Here, air flowing through plastic tubing under pressure smoothly changes switches at speeds that can be regulated from a swift snap to slow motion. We reasoned that since Lionel switches snap instantly and we were used to hearing and seeing the snap, we probably ought to stick with the twin-solenoid type.

The twin-solenoid switch machine is small and relatively easy to mount

beneath the layout. A linkage device designed and sold by Earl R. Eshleman simplifies the installation and operation further. Another advantage of this type of machine is the accessory contacts (or blades), which change indicator or signal lights in conjunction with the routing of the switch when wired appropriately. Throughout the freight yard we installed Walthers' two-light dwarf signals and Right-Of-Way's lighted brass switch stands. The dwarf signals are used to regulate the movement of trains in the yards, while the switchstands' red or green targets indicate the position of switches. All are electrically activated by the twin-solenoid machine's accessory contacts.

Two momentary-on pushbuttons operate each switch machine: one for normal alignment, the other for reversed. The three switch machine wires (one common, one from each solenoid) are routed to a terminal strip and attached there with spade lugs. From the terminal strip, two of the wires (the ones from each solenoid) are sent to the control panel

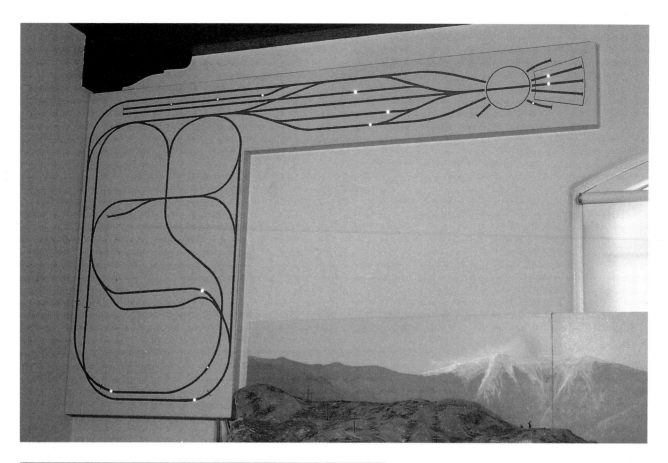

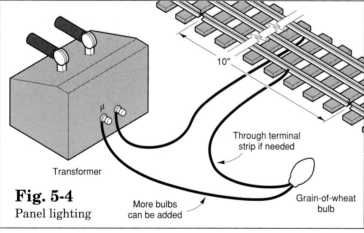

Fig. 5-4
Panel lighting

Transformer

10"

Through terminal
strip if needed

More bulbs
can be added

Grain-of-wheat
bulb

pushbutton, where they're soldered to one of the appropriate button's posts. Each button's second post wire (to complete the circuit) is looped and soldered from button to button, then routed back to the common transformer power connection, as shown in fig. 5-3. The common power third wire for the switch machine is wired from machine to machine, then back to the transformer. The machine's power requirement is about 14 to 18 volts AC/DC, and 18 gage wire is sufficient to handle the current load.

CENTRAL TRAFFIC CONTROL—CTC

GarGraves track with its wood ties gave us the opportunity to use one of the outside rails to operate CTC panel lights and other electrical signals. While this display doesn't really perform any operational function, it's fun for visitors to follow the movement of trains by looking up at the CTC panel. Cutting two gaps about 10" apart in one of the outside rails insulates that length of rail from the common current. A wire is soldered to this gapped rail, then down to a terminal strip below the layout to be further routed to a tiny "grain-of-wheat" bulb mounted in the CTC panel. The other wire lead from the bulb is "common" and again looped from bulb to bulb in the panel, then back to the transformer. Less than 8 volts of power momentarily turns the bulb on, then off as train wheels pass over the gapped rail. Remember, on three-rail equipment wheels are not insulated from each other because the metal axle is an electrical conductor between the two outside rails. The wheels act as a switch closing a circuit. See fig. 5-4. If a car or locomotive is temporarily parked in one of these CTC sections of track, the light will remain on until the car or locomotive is moved. Looking at the display, one can instantly see which tracks, sidings, or spurs are occupied as the bulbs blink on or off.

IN CONCLUSION

With a little practice the discipline of turning blocks on or off and aligning switches becomes automatic. Distractions while running the trains have to be ignored, much like distractions encountered while driving your car on a busy highway. You have to keep your hand on the throttle and your eyes on the tracks ahead. The JL/ATSF Railway is definitely a hands-on railroad with plenty of action, and it's possible to have as many as ten people run trains simultaneously from five throttles located at two separate control panels.

Cab Control

If you want to run more than one train at a time on the same track, the easiest, most economical method is cab control.

Rather than dividing a layout into sections of track where each section is electrically insulated from the next and has its own transformer (section control), cab control requires only one transformer (cab) for each train you run.

Track is divided electrically into blocks to be turned on by toggle switches at each cab's control panel. Their placement on the panel's layout schematic indicates the actual block of track that they control.

In its simplest form, the toggle switch is of the SPST (single pole, single throw) type, which turns off (open) one of the transformer's (cab) leads to the block, causing it to become electrically dead. Obviously, a train already in that block of track can't budge until the toggle switch handle is moved to the on (closed) position; nor can a train approaching from an adjacent block enter it. Much like turning room lights on and off in a darkened house, trains can run only in those rooms (blocks) where the lights are on.

To increase the capability of this basic cab control system, a second cab can be added to the same panel. This second transformer will share the panel's toggle switches if they are changed to the DPDT (double pole, double throw) center-off type. The DPDT toggle is used to wire each block using only one side of the switch. The track wire lead fastens to the center post, each transformer's lead to one of the outer posts above and below it. When it is wired in this manner, you can turn on the block from either transformer simply by flipping the toggle switch to the left or right of center. Use the other side of the toggle's posts to wire panel indicator lamps, showing which blocks are in use.

Here's how it works in actual operation:

As a train is run from one of the transformers, simply flip the toggle toward that cab sometime before the train enters the block; flip it back to center after the train leaves it. This way the unoccupied blocks can be used by the other transformer and its train by flipping the toggles toward that cab. As both trains move about, you flip toggle switches as necessary, and neither train ever has to share the same transformer. To handle more trains, move to another layout location and add another control panel with two more cabs. Once again either transformer can run its train in any block.

Flexibility: Cab control also permits section control or continuous running just by flipping on the appropriate toggles to cover the desired sequence of blocks to be run from a cab. Specific information about cab control is presented in great detail in the book *Your Guide to Easy Model Railroad Wiring* by Andy Sperandeo (Kalmbach Publishing Co., no. 12093).

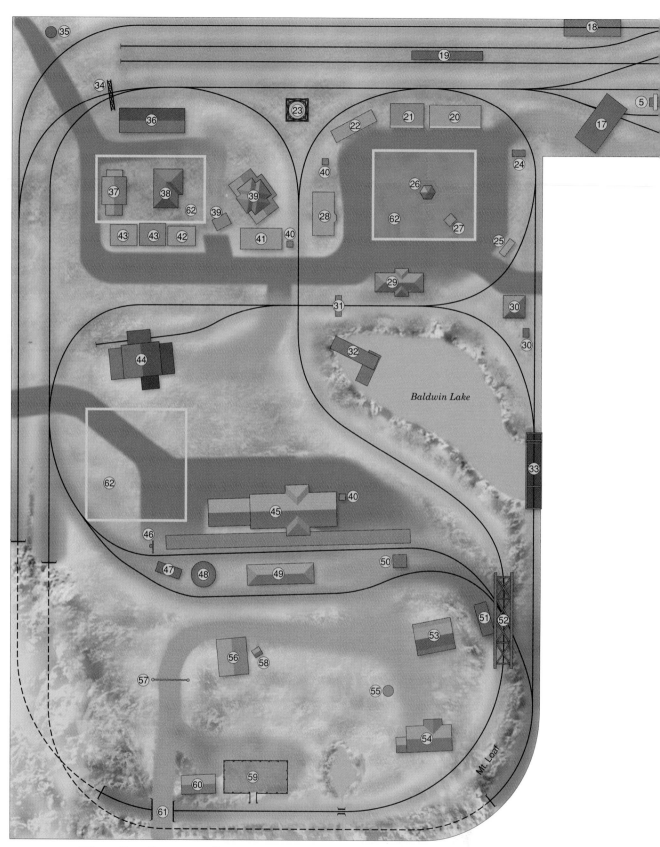

Fig. 5-5. Track plan and structure key of the JL/ATSF Railway

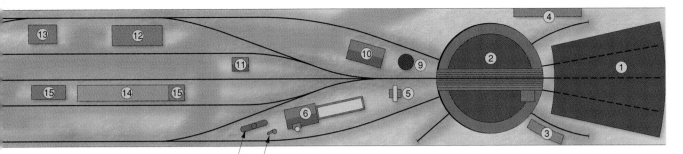

1. Roundhouse (Korber model, similar to AT&SF Bakersfield, Calif.)

2. Turntable (Bowser, similar to AT&SF Bakersfield, Calif.)

3. Service platform (scratchbuilt, plans in 1950 *Lionel Bantam Book*)

4. Concrete loading platform (scratchbuilt)

5. Yard light towers (Lionel)

6. Sand house (Korber model)

7. Water column

8. Fuel tank (Lionel O-27 tank car body)

9. Fuel tank (Engineering Model Assoc.) (Plastruct)

10. Freight shed (Lionel)

11. Storage shed for flags, fusees, etc.

12. Icing platform (Lionel working accessory)

13. Control tower (Lionel working accessory)

14. Lumber mill (Lionel working accessory)

15. Lumber sheds (Lionel)

16. Yardmaster's office (Thomas Yorke model)

17. Young's coaling station (Lionel)

18. Diesel and passenger car washstand (scratchbuilt)

19. Diesel fueling station (scratchbuilt)

20. Bank building (Design Preservation Models Lunde Landmarks)

21. CL Walker Building (Design Preservation Models Lunde Landmarks)

22. Pete and Joe's Diner (K-Lineville)

23. Water tower (Lionel)

24. JoAnn's fruit stand (Selley)

25. Oil pump (Boomtown Models)

26. Plaza bandstand (scratchbuilt)

27. Leo Nell (scratchbuilt statue)

28. Texaco gas station (Bachmann Plasticville)

29. Molino Depot and platform (Lionel)

30. Highland Junction tower and telephone hut (Bachmann)

31. Platform across tracks to Baldwin Lake steps and beach

32. Motor boat pier with boathouse and Lionel Barrel House

33. Bascule bridge (Lionel working accessory)

34. Signal bridge (Bachmann with Walthers operating signals)

35. Water tank (35mm film canister)

36. Thrasher Bros. warehouse (Thomas Yorke model)

37. 2-Story residence (Plasticville)

38. 1-Story ranch-type residence (Plasticville)

39. 2-Story California Craftsman cottage and garage (scratchbuilt)

40. Telephone booths (Mountain States Model Works)

41. Every Nite Inn (Plasticville Motel)

42. F&H Hardware (K-Lineville)

43. Post office, barber shop, bakery, (K-Lineville)

44. Lesser Bros. Purina Chows (Lionel)

45. Cucamonga Depot (Lionel-Rico Station)

46. Cantilever signal bridge (scratchbuilt)

47. Kinko's trailer (retired AT&SF superintendent) (Plasticville mobile home)

48. Water tower (Lionel)

49. Freight station (Lionel)

50. Hand car shed (Thomas Yorke model)

51. Hobo car (Lionel boxcar shell)

52. Truss bridge (Lionel)

53. Barn and silo (Bachmann-Plasticville)

54. Ranch house and yard (Plasticville)

55. Windmill and open water tank (Plasticville)

56. Grandpa's shack (Thomas Yorke model)

57. Main gate Circle L Ranch (scratchbuilt)

58. Grandpa's outhouse

59. Cattle loading pen (scratchbuilt)

60. Summit freight platform (Bachmann)

61. Auto bridge leading to Ranch and Summit (scratchbuilt)

62. Access hatches

6 Scenery

AS MODEL RAILROADERS, we often do things backwards—sometimes even by intent! The best example of a planned reversal is scenery construction. Unlike the real world, the mountains, plains, and waterways on our layouts are created after the rail lines have traversed them, and we're left to fill those in-between spaces however we choose.

The best time to begin thinking about our railroad's scenic environment is when we start planning the layout. Too often, in our haste to get trains up and running, we build benchwork, lay down roadbed and track, and then think about what the landscape should look like and where we'll put those structures we've already bought or built. Regrettably, we end up having to leave out industries that are supposed to create traffic on our railroad, or we're forced into making scenic choices so improbable they fail to look at all convincing. Granted, there is a prototype for practically everything, but we ought to be modeling the ordinary, not the extraordinary.

As mentioned in Chapter 2, construction of the JL/ATSF Railway progressed in a sequence of zones devised during the planning stage. Furthermore, the three-dimensional layout mock-up helped us enormously; we could see ahead of time how the desired Southern California scenic setting could be incorporated to complement the final track plan. After making the appropriate refinements, we began our scenic efforts in the freight yard.

THE FREIGHT YARD

To give the freight yard a prototypical dirty, sandy look, we covered the entire area with a mix of Highball Products cinder, iron ore, and dark gray ballasts blended together and secured with the same solution of matte medium used to ballast track. Real tan-colored dirt, sifted to remove pebbles,

simulates the yard's dirt access roads. All structures, including the turntable bridge and pit modified to look more "Santa Fe," are weathered to represent the buildup of grime and grease common to real yards. Because the yard is quite narrow, we needed to provide some sort of visual illusion to increase its depth, as well as to give the entire layout a sense of continuing beyond the living room walls. This was realistically resolved with a tempered Masonite backdrop painted by local artist Pony Horton with acrylic paints. It depicts Southern California from the nearby railroad yards all the way out to the distant tips of the hazy mountain ranges and passes.

SUMMIT

Summit and the Circle L Ranch are located in the mountainous region of the JL/ATSF Railway that can be reached only after penetrating a short, curved tunnel. Beneath this

FACING PAGE: Scenery—it's the stage of development where a toy train layout begins to take on noticeable Hi-rail characteristics. Lots of details are involved, of course, but the dusty, sandy look of the freight yard contributes a lot to the feel of Southern California railroading. Service roads in the freight yard, for example, are real tan-colored dirt.

BELOW: Structures are part of the scenery, too. The turntable pit and roundhouse, for instance, are weathered to represent grime typically found in the area of enginehouses.

Fig. 6-1. Masonite profile contours reinforce and control the terrain's shape. Masking tape and newspaper support the hardshell scenery that follows.

Fig. 6-2. If you want your scenery to be realistic, don't forget to line the insides of your tunnels. The authors used black cardboard. If you ignore this detail, a few inches of tunnel interior will show, revealing masking tape and the underside of the tinted hardshell.

high plateau, the rail line to Cucamonga passes through a much longer tunnel. This double elevation of stacked tracks required careful planning and some of the aforementioned reverse engineering. The solution here, we decided, was to build the mountains and the high plateau using the well-documented hardshell technique, which would leave the area underneath it open for easy access to the lower track whenever maintenance is required. To reinforce and control the terrain's shape, we cut Masonite profile contours duplicating heavy, brown paper templates drawn in place, then permanently fastened them to the benchwork (fig. 6-1).

Prior to covering the Summit and Circle L Ranch area, we installed

tunnel portals built from balsa, scored and painted to look like poured concrete, then lined them with black cardboard curved lengthwise and extending several inches back from each portal's mouth. See fig. 6-2. This effectively blocked any light leaks from the open expanse beneath the layout and the hardshell covering above it.

With the initial paper towel and Hydrocal covering set hard, we applied a second, heavier coat of molding plaster that was lightly tinted with powdered brown pigment (available from art stores). See fig. 6-3. Molding plaster takes a while to harden and is easy to work when carving rock strata and terrain details. The colored pigment maintains the basic earth throughout the plaster form and won't show white if accidentally chipped. Final texturing of

the entire plastered area is done by wetting the plaster with a mist of spray-bottled water, then dusting it with dry, tinted molding plaster tapped onto it through a fine-meshed strainer. This technique, known as Zip-texturing and made popular by Linn Westcott in the 1950s, leaves the plaster surface coarse when dry.

All plaster on the JL/ATSF Railway is colored with multiple applications of Rit dye mixed in water, then spray-bottled onto its surface. Rit dye (powder or liquid) is readily available in fabric stores and supermarkets in a wide assortment of colors, and it's nontoxic. Dissolved in water, colors can be mixed in a variety of strengths. We found that repeated applications of weak—rather than strong— solutions gave us better control of the color; besides, it's a lot easier to add

Fig. 6-3. Plaster tinted with powdered brown pigment gives a basic earth tone

Fig. 6-4. Black Rit dye sprayed over rock strata realistically darkens crevices.

Fig. 6-5. Ground covering applied over the tinted plaster is the final texturing step.

than to remove color. It's a good idea to mix several tans, browns, a rust, a black, and shades of green in different spray bottles, having them ready to mist on as you see fit. Save black for last to darken crevices in carved rock strata, as shown in fig. 6-4. Some modelers who use fluorescent fixtures without UV filters have found that their dye coloring fades. The JL/ATSF Railway uses incandescent lighting, and we haven't noticed any fading in five years. This might be an argument for incandescent lighting. Woodland Scenics ground covering sprinkled on over the colored plaster (fig. 6-5) does a credible job of representing typical Southern California vegetation.

Water in Summit Creek, the Circle L Ranch livestock basin, and draining from culverts at various locations throughout the layout is two-part casting resin poured in layers. The dirt road at Summit that leads to the depot and further to the ranch is, again, real dirt chosen for its color and

Scenery Methods and Materials

As modelers we tend to model what we like best, and the methods and materials we use are almost as varied as the places we model. Usually there isn't just one way to achieve an adequate result—it's more a matter of combining several methods and materials to accomplish superior results. Here are some of the most popular techniques and materials.

SCREEN WIRE AND PLASTER: A method that's been around for years, it still works well. Contour hillside formers made from scrap material (such as wood, plywood, or Masonite) are first attached to the benchwork, then covered with screening tacked or stapled to them. (Aluminum screening is more pliable than steel.) Any popular plaster (i.e., Structolite by U.S. Gypsum is lightweight and easily workable) is spread over the screen wire, resulting in scenery that is exceptionally strong and must be sawed apart when making changes.

NEWSPAPER, PAPER TOWELS, AND HYDROCAL: Pioneered by the late Linn Westcott in the 1950s, it remains one of the most popular methods. Terrain is shaped by piling up loosely balled newspaper, then weaving masking tape back and forth over it, creating a web that helps define contours. Misting with water from a spray bottle easily tames the springiness of the paper and helps everything behave.

When the desired contours have been established, paper towels are dipped in a soupy mix of water and Hydrocal plaster (another U.S. Gypsum product) and draped, blanketlike, over the damp newspaper and tape. Hydrocal is a very hard, dense plaster, much stronger than patching plaster or plaster of Paris. When the paper toweling dries, the structural properties of Hydrocal allow the newspaper and tape to be removed from underneath it (if desired) leaving a "hardshell," the term coined by Westcott for this type of scenery construction. Hardshell scenery has the advantage of being very light in weight. It can be quickly changed by cutting out the desired area and replacing it with a newly contoured one.

CARDBOARD STRIPS AND HYDROCAL: Another way to contour the landscape is to build forms with cardboard strips. Long strips of cardboard are cut, then glued and stapled to the benchwork in a basketlike weave. Shapes are changed by cutting and restapling strips or adding more of them. After the basic countours are built, they're covered with paper towels dipped in Hydrocal just as described in the preceding paragraph. Along with light weight, another advantage of hardshell is greater contour control.

GAUZE AND HYDROCAL: An alternative to plaster-dipped towels is plaster-impregnated gauze, a material used by doctors to make casts for broken bones. The gauze is merely dipped in water and placed in position as before. Its greatest advantage is its neatness, but cost can be a consideration on larger layouts. Carried by some hobby shops under the Paris-Craft or Woodland Scenics brand name, it can also be purchased from art supply and craft stores.

STYROFOAM: The past decade has seen a large increase in modelers using extruded Styrofoam insulating panels as a scenery base. Available at lumberyards and home centers, its greatest virtues are its near weightlessness and its toughness, making it the ideal material for modular and portable layouts or dioramas.

To make terrain contours with Styrofoam, you build it up in layers glued together with a water-based cement, then carve, shape, and smooth off the edges with a serrated knife, rasp, and Sur-Form tool (Stanley makes a good one) until the desired contour is achieved. Some modelers also use a Hot-Wire tool in the shaping process.

The most controllable of methods, Styrofoam's disadvantages are its high cost and the slowness of the work. On larger layouts, don't overlook the possibility of Styrofoam as the ideal scenery material to cover removable access hatches.

sifted free of impurities. Real pebbles glued together with white glue form the protective and decorative barriers on either side of the Circle L's drive.

BALDWIN LAKE

Baldwin Lake is the inverse of Summit; whereas Summit's topography goes up, Baldwin Lake's goes down. The techniques employed to build each are essentially the same. The lake has, however, the distinction of being the last zone to be scenicked. It's a simple explanation, really. Like the proverbial painter who's careful not to paint himself into a corner, Baldwin Lake is the place in the benchwork that had to remain open until last so that Cucamonga Depot and the Town of Molino could be completed.

Baldwin Lake had to have sufficient depth to make the Lionel bascule bridge located at one end of it believable. For the sake of an interesting scenic effect, we built one side of the lake much like an aquarium that visitors to the layout, especially children, could look into. Working this concept through, Baldwin Lake became a hardshell bathtub colored and detailed to look like a lake bottom. See fig. 6-6. Tinting is pale blue-green near the surface, darkening to a much deeper blue at the bottom. Since the water was to be rippled Plexiglas, all the surface water details (fig. 6-7) had to be planned in advance, so that their submerged parts could be modeled separately. Then the Plexiglas water surface was sandwiched between them and the upper parts of the same details. Once we accomplished this and the Plexiglas was in place, we landscaped the lake's banks—another

Fig. 6-6. The bottom of Baldwin Lake is scenicked just like the rest of the layout, except that it's concave.

Fig. 6-7. Surface—and subsurface—details had to be taken care of in advance. For instance, the sailboat's hull was halved lengthwise, then glued to the underside of the Plexiglas, furthering the illusion of real water in Baldwin Lake.

Fig. 6-8. With the Plexiglas water in place, landscaping the lake's banks finished the scene

case of reverse engineering (fig. 6-8). The final touch was to seal the viewing window at the front of the layout. This was easily done with a smooth piece of smoked Plexiglas cut to size, butted up against the rippled Plexiglas, then screwed in place. The ability to look into a lake from above or below is a fun feature seldom modeled and one sure to draw comment. Try it!

Additional scenery construction references we suggest are: *How to Build Realistic Model Railroad Scenery*, by Dave Frary (Kalmbach Publishing Co., no. 12100), and *The Scenery Manual* by Woodland Scenics. Both are of great help in realistic railroading with toy trains.

Stretching Space

The trouble with model trains is that they're limited by space. Much as we'd wish, we can't physically duplicate the stretching-to-the-horizon mainline tracks of the real thing, but we can create that illusion. Consider the following scenic devices you can implement for stretching space.

BACKDROPS: When one or more sides of the layout butt against a wall, the wall can be covered with backdrop material (tempered Masonite is a popular choice), then painted to add apparent depth to the scene. Paint, rolled, brushed, or airbrushed on to simulate sky and clouds will, by itself, begin to increase distance. Add some painted topography, such as nearby hills and not-so-nearby mountains, and the illusion is further enhanced. If you don't care to paint backdrops yourself, there are numerous commercial ones available from several different companies. Most are made of paper and are applied much like wallpaper. Designed to overlap, a long, continuous scenic panorama is possible, or sections can be cut apart to satisfy a confined area. A good source for finding out what's currently available is the annual Walther's catalog available at your local train hobby shop. Some enterprising modelers have also successfully used cutouts from scenic calendar photography as backdrop paste-ups.

FLATS: Three-dimensional hills or mountains built up to painted continuations on the backdrop add considerable depth to a scene, providing that joints are properly blended or hidden. Sometimes, however, the space available between track and wall is too confined to permit this approach. In that case, profile flats (1/4" Masonite, plywood, Fome-Cor, etc.) cut to contours representing rolling hills or mountain ranges can be placed two or three deep, putting the lowest in front and the highest closest to the backdrop. Very little separation is required between them to create a three-dimensional effect of looking at a series of progressively higher and more distant ranges. In urban areas, city or industrial building flats built as a single wall against an appropriately painted backdrop will lend sufficient depth to again create the illusion of three-dimensional structures.

MIRRORS: Large and small mirrors are excellent space stretchers when care is taken in their placement. Reflected scenes and details are wrong at a rakish angle, right when the image is a continued one; of course, you don't want to be able to see yourself. A mirrored scene continuation can be further enhanced by using reversed lettering on the backs of signs or buildings so that their reflected image will be normal and readable. Mirrors are most easily concealed in urban scenes where their tops and sides are hidden by overpasses and building walls.

VIEW BLOCKS: A free-standing island layout where none of the sides butt against the wall can be made to look larger if a portion of it is divided by a false double-faced backdrop that blocks a complete overview of the layout from either side. This block need only be as high as necessary to prevent looking over it to the other side. Again using Masonite, plywood, or Fome-Cor, each side will be painted to continue the scene leading to it. These scenes can be as different as, for example, urban on one side and rural on the other, thereby effectively creating the illusion of a layout twice its actual size.

More information: These general ideas about stretching space are applicable to any layout. More specific information about these devices and countless other scenic techniques can be found in the book *Scenery for Model Railroaders* (Kalmbach Books, no. 12008).

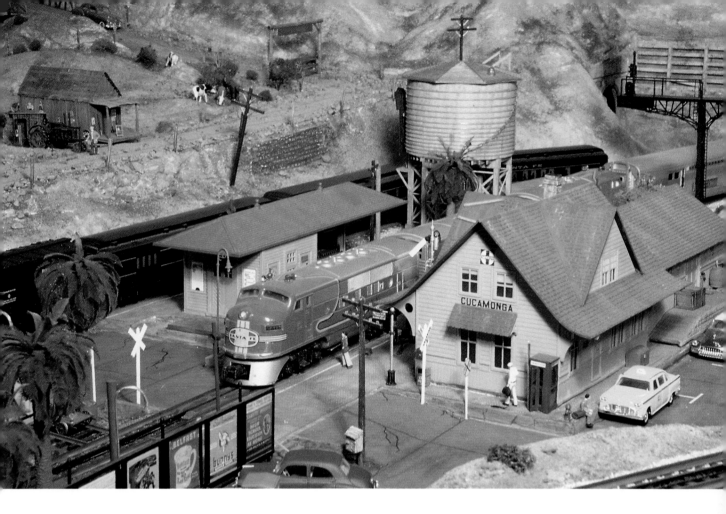

7 Structures

AT ITS SIMPLEST, a railroad is two narrow ribbons of steel running between points. In between, or at its terminus, it passes through towns, cities, industries, and yards, branching into additional ribbons of steel that form a network. The purpose of this network of rails is to move goods and people from point to point.

Since people and freight are involved, structures become an integral part of the railroad network as they protect goods and people from the elements, store equipment, function as service facilities, and provide offices and other places of business for the railroads.

Like their prototypes, model structures come in all shapes and sizes and can be built from many different materials. Most model railroaders build structures from kits. Two good sources for the latest O scale structure-kit information are the latest Oakridge Corporation O scale buyer's guide and Walthers O & S scale catalog. Stop by your local train

What a feast for model railroading eyes! The color and detail in this scene depicting the *Super Chief* pulling into Cucamonga station are terrific. Cucamonga Station's origin is, of course, Lionel's Rico Station kit; both the freight station and the water tower are repainted Lionel accessories.

hobby shop; while they can't carry everything, what is there is often a good representation of what's currently on the market. And if kits aren't enough, check out the remarkable number of parts available for use in scratchbuilding structures. By far the most common material used today for building structures from scratch is styrene.

If you feel you're not quite ready for this more-advanced phase of the hobby, consider building a kit. A sizable number of plastic kits can be built exactly as they come out of the box and look acceptable on the layout. Or take it one step further and have a building that's different from the next guy's simply by adding a little paint. A nice paint job can work miracles on a straight-from-the-box kit. You can also leave off some details or change, add, or move others

to create a structure that better fits the needs and look of your layout.

You can also combine parts of several kits to "kitbash" a structure of your own design or to approximate a favorite prototype building. The possibilities are almost endless, and the flexibility in building structures makes them really enjoyable modeling projects. Here are but three examples on the JL/ATSF Railway. Rather than copy these, learn from the techniques and build structures of your own design.

CUCAMONGA STATION

Like all structures on the JL/ATSF Railway, Cucamonga Station has undergone physical and cosmetic changes. It began as a Lionel Rico Station plastic kit (based on the Rio Grande Southern depot still standing in Colorado)—at first glance, at least, a far cry from anything remotely resembling prototypical Santa Fe. However, upon further review . . . not so! If you were to compare the kit contents against photos of actual Santa Fe depots, you'd find that only minor changes are necessary to make it look like a Santa Fe station. Here's the process.

We relegated all decorative roof and gable trim pieces to our "stuff" box. The tower pieces met the same fate. Next, we assembled the station according to the kit's instructions and painted its exterior a prototypical Santa Fe Colonial Yellow (1 part Floquil S.P. Armour Yellow, 1 part Floquil Reefer White) and its roof Santa Fe Venetian Red (Floquil Zinc Chromate), colors appropriate to our era.

Deciding to light the interior of the telegrapher's bay window, we taped a clear 14-volt grain-of-wheat bulb to the inside of the roof, making sure that the bulb's leads were long enough to extend down through a hole in the table, where they could be connected to the appropriate accessory bus wires. Not wanting the interior light to shine through other station windows (in reality not all interior building lights are turned on at the same time), we closed off the inside of the bay window area with cardboard walls cut and glued to fit. All windows then received window shades cut from masking tape pressed onto their clear plastic panes. We staggered these to model shades realistically pulled down to different lengths.

(Note also in the photos that we—brace yourselves, collectors—painted Lionel accessories to fit into the scene. We were surprised how good some of them looked.)

The interior assembly and modification complete, we added a couple of balsa boards to the part of the roof

Attention to details, like the masking tape window shades in the upstairs windows, make the difference between a ho-hum and a "wow" scene.

once covered by the tower, where it was devoid of shingles. This subtle touch is a characteristic of actual building roofs that have undergone structural modification.

Because potbellied stoves were common to depots of the era we were modeling, we decided it would be fun to have a smoking chimney. We measured the inside dimensions of the kit's brick chimney and fit a Seuthe smoke unit into it, extending the smoke unit's wire leads through a hole in the table beneath the station. Before joining the leads to the accessory bus wires, we connected them to a variable resistor from Radio Shack. The resistor enables us to regulate the voltage going to the smoke unit and, therefore, the amount of smoke it produces. It's a real eye-catcher when fired up!

Before lightly weathering the entire structure, we added to both ends of the depot typical Santa Fe heralds and decals spelling "Cucamonga."

This identifies the location and the railroad being served. A helpful tip: when you build your own layout, do everything you can to identify the location you're modeling (general or specific) and the time period. More on this later.

Lastly, appropriate signage (available from Vintage Reproductions), including Railway Express and Western Union signs glued to the exterior walls and a signpost where they appeared in our research photographs, was the finishing touch.

The Rico Station kit returned to the JL/ATSF Railway as Cucamonga Station, a fascinating caterpillar-to-butterfly transformation! Pretty nifty, wouldn't you agree?

FREIGHT YARD SAWMILL

The operating sawmill located on one of the freight yard tracks is Lionel's no. 12873 repainted, detailed, and weathered. We felt it would be nice to expand the basic structure by

The freight yard sawmill is a logical grouping of repainted Lionel kits.

adding two Lionel no. 12705 lumber sheds, one on each end. These are painted to match the sawmill, then further detailed with stacks of banded board lumber, a workbench, and the kinds of figures and vehicles one would expect to find in a lumber-yard. This grouping of reworked Lionel structures is a good example of how easily a little paint and logical detailing can favorably alter the out-of-the-box toy look of these products.

MOLINO'S TEXACO STATION
Available from K-Line as an inex-pensive plastic kit, this typical 1950s gas station looks gaudy and toylike if built as is. With only a little modifi-cation here and there, however, it can look like the real thing.

Part of making it look like the real thing, of course, involved legwork.

After Texaco had kindly provided period graphics, artwork, and photo-graphy, (see Chapter 10), recon-struction began. The first step was to paint the insides of all walls Floquil Reefer Gray to eliminate the trans-lucent quality of the white plastic. This would keep the entire structure from glowing should we decide to add interior lighting.

The next step was to paint the Art Deco trim, garage doors, service bay signs, and other details Floquil Dark Green, the color appropriate, once again, to the 1940s and '50s. Clear .015" styrene sheet (from Evergreen Models at your local hobby shop) cut to size and then glued behind all win-dow openings with plastic cement served nicely as window panes.

Before installing the one-piece plastic roof, we painted it Floquil

Details added are banded board lum-ber, trucks, a fork-lift, and for the human element, people.

63

ABOVE: This K-Line Gas Station kit is altered and detailed to match Texaco stations of the 1940s and '50s, right down to the Coke machine and half-tire border.

RIGHT: Actual Texaco Station photographs show how the gas islands should be modeled.

Weathered Black, and when this had dried, drew irregular "tar" lines with a fine Sharpie pen to complete the look of a tar-papered surface. With the roof glued in place and the structure-part of the gas station finished, the gas islands and car lift came next. The pumps were repainted red and silver with black hoses. We cut pump "crowns" from Selley Models pumps of that era, then painted and glued them to the tops of the plastic pumps. To finish up, we painted the oil can racks, the molded cans, and the service island bases (Floquil Concrete). Then we weathered the car lift to show lots of grease and oil. Even the figures supplied in the kit now wear authentic Texaco uniforms, right up to the once-famous star on their caps!

Finished, the gas station and service islands are now glued in place on their concrete apron (balsa painted with Floquil Concrete), and details including tires, a Coke machine, Coke bottles, and a gum-ball machine are placed alongside the structure wherever they appeared in the photos of actual Texaco stations.

WEATHERING

Most plastic structures look more realistic after you give them a coat of Testor's Dullcote from an aerosol spray can. Dullcote, which is a clear, flat lacquer, flattens the gloss of painted plastic and gives it a less toylike, more natural, appearance. Look around you; in real life you seldom see bright, shiny structures. Weather takes a toll on them (hence the term, "weathering"), with dirt, soot, grime, rust, and oxidation wreaking eventual havoc on paint or galvanized metal.

We can simulate the ravages of weather by adding thin washes of paint to our model. Floquil Polly S water-based acrylic paints are free of solvents that can craze plastic (or you can use regular Floquil enamels if you first coat the plastic with Floquil Barrier), and the weathering effects can be washed or wiped off before the paint dries if it doesn't look right. Look at real buildings to see how dirt and fading affect structures. Sometimes mud splashes up and dirt washes down. Soot tends to build up around smokestacks, over tunnel portals, even engine or roundhouse doors like a dusting. Just remember to work most weathering effects vertically, since that is how rain washes the prototype. A tip when using acrylic washes: a small drop of household liquid dishwashing detergent added to the water will break the surface tension and make the acrylic wash flow better.

Thin washes aren't the only method for weathering structures. Dry pigment and chalk powder (both available from art supply stores, the latter scraped from colored chalk pastel sticks with a knife) can be applied with a soft brush, then sealed with a light spray of Dullcote.

Dry-brushing is a technique with a name that describes it. Primarily used for highlighting, dry-brushing requires a broad, stiff-bristled brush. Simply dip the tip of the brush in your paint (usually a light color), brush most of the paint out of the bristles onto a piece of paper toweling, and then swiftly brush up and down the area you're trying to highlight with the almost-dry brush. The technique is very effective if done with a light touch.

Structures are an integral part of any model railroad. Choose them carefully, and don't be afraid to repaint, weather, or otherwise modify them to make them more realistically meet your needs.

Thrasher Warehouse is a good example of a weathered and detailed structure. Its corrugated aluminum roof definitely belongs to the era modeled.

8 Details Along the Right-of-Way

TO OUR WAY OF THINKING, it's at this point that the differences between a toy train layout and a Hi-rail layout begin to be magnified. It's the small things that set a Hi-rail layout apart from the standard track-on-painted-plywood pike. If realism is what you hope to achieve with your layout, realism really begins here. In this chapter, we'll focus on right-of-way details that are easy to make—details that make a difference. We'll describe some of the trackside items we built; many of them will probably be appropriate for your own layout. Those that aren't? Well, perhaps you can learn something from the techniques and materials we've used.

Where do you get ideas for detailing your layout? If you're modeling a contemporary railroad, your task isn't all that difficult. A few trips down to the main line, freight yard, or depot (if it's still there), will reveal objects that can be modeled easily.

If you're modeling earlier days along the main line, your task is going to be a little more difficult. Many of the details once commonplace on American railroads no longer survive. Sure, they were there in the 1930s and '40s, but like the disappearance of the steam locomotive, the caboose, the water tank, the coaling tower, the roundhouse, and so many other romantic and nostalgic reminders of the past, they are gone. You can draw upon your memory, of course, but as time passes most of us find this to be increasingly unreliable.

A really excellent source that overcomes the failure of our gray matter is the multitude of photographic railroad books on today's market. Railroad photos from the steam era, for example, weren't ordinarily taken to accentuate right-of-way details. But if you play detective a little bit, searching beyond the three-quarter view of the locomotive, you'll start to see less-obvious aspects of the photos. Often, interesting details can be found hidden in the background, around locomotives in freight yards, at depots, or on the main line, just as if we were actually able to travel back in time.

In the initial heavy construction stages of a layout, we're not concerned with building and placing such lineside details. In fact, it's dangerous to install them on a layout too soon because they're likely to be damaged. Trust us—there will be times when you just don't feel like getting into a long construction session. Those are great times to pull out your railroad books and look for right-of-way details. You can build a few of them now and then and keep them safely tucked away until a section of the layout nears completion and they can be put in place permanently without fear of destruction.

A PORTABLE STAIRCASE

To service, clean, or repair locomotives and rolling stock, railroad workers have to climb up and scramble all over them. Stepladders are

FACING PAGE: Details not only add believability to a Hi-rail layout, they become a point of focus. By observing real-life details along the railroad—objects like whistle posts and rail racks—and then modeling them on your layout, you'll add lots of interest to your pike.

BELOW: Portable staircases can be found almost anywhere in the yard. This brightly painted example is in position to service a yard switcher.

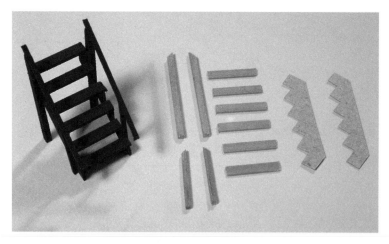

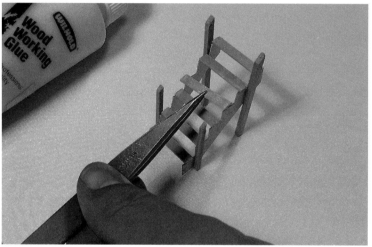

Mark and cut the different-size balsa strips—first the two step risers, then the railings, and finally six 4-foot-long steps (1" in O scale) as shown in fig. 8-1.

After you've cut all the pieces, begin to assemble them. For this type of assembly, wood glue (e.g., Franklin Titebond) is best, as it dries pretty quickly. Assemble the vertical supports to the handrailing, then to the risers. Carefully glue the top and bottom steps in place so that the staircase will stand, then glue the remaining steps where they belong. Use tweezers (fig. 8-2) to hold small pieces in place for a couple of seconds while the glue sets. You may want to build several staircases concurrently. This saves time, and you'll probably want more than one, anyway. Once the staircase is assembled, it's ready to be painted. The color should—for obvious safety reasons—be bright and highly visible; we used Floquil Signal Red.

PLACING TRACKSIDE DETAILS

Placement of trackside details on the layout is important. Naturally, you want to be able to readily see and enjoy what you've painstakingly reproduced. After all, that's one of the main reasons you spent so much time building that structure, mini-scene, or lineside detail. So why then should you put a lighted, detailed, weathered signal or structure somewhere way toward the back of the layout where no one will be able to appreciate your craftsmanship? Good question. Maybe you *shouldn't* put that signal there. Maybe you have another signal—perhaps one of lesser quality—that could be placed there. The point is, something needs to be there simply because in real life it *would* be there. Viewers will recognize that

Fig. 8-1 (TOP). Pieces of balsa have been cut for the two staircase risers, steps, and railings.

Fig. 8-2 (ABOVE). A pair of tweezers makes gluing the steps to the risers a somewhat easier task. Vertical posts are already in place.

fine for small jobs, but a portable staircase is even handier when it comes to performing light maintenance and conducting periodic inspections. Moved into position by four people or by forklift, a staircase is a whole lot easier to climb than a ladder, especially when the worker is carrying tools and doesn't have a spare hand. It's also a safer place to work from.

We used balsa to build the staircase. Good sizes for the uprights are 1/8" by 1/16" strips. Railings are 1/8" square, risers 1/16" x 1/2", and steps 1/8" x 3/16" x 1" long. Decide how high you want your stairs. We measured a couple of steam locomotives and found that to reach their running boards (or cab windows on diesels), a height of 6½ scale feet is correct, and a scale 4-foot-long step is adequate.

something is missing, and the impact of realism you've gained will be diminished. In the case of the JL/ATSF Railway, after a little digging, we came across a couple of scale target signals used on an earlier layout. They are inoperable and have their backs facing the front of the layout, but they look perfect in the background, facing away from any viewer.

On a real railroad, there are points of concentrated activity, where details can often be found in clusters. Of course, on a model railroad you're working in a small space to begin with, so details tend to be even closer together than they are in real life. The photo at the beginning of this chapter shows a surprising amount of detail in a 7-square-inch area. There are signs for the engineer to blow his locomotive's whistle or horn to announce his approach to a station and another advising him of the station ahead. Here too, we built an easy detail piece, called a "rail rack," used to store spare rails for emergencies.

RAIL RACK

A couple of 3-foot lengths of O scale rail purchased at a local hobby shop are all you need to build this detail.

Determine about how high off the ground these rails should be, then cut two upright supports, adding an actual ¼" to anchor them in the layout surface. Use a motor tool and cutting disk as described earlier to cut the rails. Cut a couple more short sections for the cross hangers. Super glue or solder will work to assemble them in a T shape. Place the completed support racks approximately 20 scale feet apart (5 actual inches). Now cut a few more lengths of rail to simulate those scale 40-footers (10") on the racks. About four of them will give the rack a realistic look. Finally, paint the racks silver or black and the rails brown to look as though they're rusted. Don't forget to throw a few spare ties around. They too are there for the track gangs.

CLEARANCE MARKER

Here's a detail that serves both a cosmetic and a practical purpose. It's simply a bright orange spot of paint on a tie—perhaps the simplest detail of all, requiring only a bottle of paint and a brush. Simple though it may be, it has a lot of impact. Visitors almost always spot it and ask: "What's that for?" Here's the explanation we

Scale rails made into T bars hold 40-foot replacement rails in position along the right-of-way for emergency use. Ties scattered here and there along the right-of-way also look right.

give: Accidents on railroads, especially in freight yards, can happen when cars left too close to converging tracks are sideswiped by another for lack of clearance. To help reduce these accidents, real railroads take bright orange paint and mark the ends of ties at the clearance limit so the switchman or engineer can easily recognize cars left protruding past the mark. It's easy to understand how this kind of an accident can occur, and it probably will sooner or later on your own layout. You can prevent it with that important little orange stripe. And remember, it's there for both safety and realism!

FISHPLATES AND TIEPLATES

No, a fishplate is neither a place setting nor a menu item at your favorite seafood restaurant. In railroad terminology, a fishplate is a piece of metal that spans the joint between two sections of rail. It serves the same function as the rail connectors Lionel provided for setting up trains on the floor; i.e., it keeps the rails from coming apart. Bolts are passed through the fishplates and rail webs, tying them together. With today's improved welded rail construction, fishplates

Another detail is tieplates—pieces of steel used to track to ties. Here the authors bought scale model tieplates and fishplates and painted them to blend rally with the surrounding area.

The authors found this heap of tieplates alongside AT&SF main line in Cajon Pass.

are used less frequently, but if you're still running steam locomotives, fishplates are commonplace, and broken ones would be found discarded all along the right-of-way. Berkshire Valley sells all kinds of neat O scale detail items. We took one of their molded plastic junk bins modeled prototypically from old rail ties and used it as a tieplate and fishplate storage area. The model tieplates and fishplates are from Grandt Line (part nos. 9001 and 9004). Combined with the junk bin, fishplates are yet another detail common to a railroad's parts inventory. Dirty up everything with paint colors that blend into the adjacent ground cover.

Pole Line Basics

Most railroads, standard or narrow gauge, provide their own lines of communication through wires strung between poles closely paralleling the tracks. Although older uninsulated wire is slowly being replaced by insulated wire (much of it placed underground), pole lines can still be seen across the country and are commonplace on all rights-of-way. Here are the four basic elements of a pole line:

POLES: Communication poles carry telephone, telegraph, and signal lines and range in height from 16 to 60 feet or more graduated in increments of 5 feet. The average span between poles is 150 feet, but this can vary with the needs or limitations of the terrain. On our model layouts it's wise to shorten the distance to whatever looks right. This will create the illusion of the tracks extending farther than if we adhered to prototype spacing.

WIRES AND CROSSARMS: Uninsulated wire run between pole lines is typically galvanized steel .109" to .168" in diameter. From pole lines to trackside telephone shanties or agents' offices, the wire is rubber-insulated, encased in heavy sheathing. The model effect is of a single line double the size of the line wire, which should run from a small metal case near the top of the pole down to a strain anchor (hook) on the side of the building, then to another small metal case below it.

Crossarms can carry as few as two and as many as ten line wires, depending on demand. They are fastened to the pole beginning about 10" from the top moving downward on 24" centers at "gains" (1" deep dado notches) cut into the pole and held in place by a 5/8" throughbolt and two 20" strap metal braces carriage-bolted to the crossarm and lagged to the pole. Threaded wooden pins project vertically 6" from the crossarms to hold insulators.

INSULATORS: Line wires attached directly to the wooden pins would, in dampness, cause short circuits and false grounds. They are, therefore, anchored to glass insulators that have internal threads to screw onto the threaded pins. Early insulators were manufactured from cheap bottle glass in colors ranging from translucent green to translucent blue, and eventually to clear as the quality of glass improved. Small glass or plastic beads are the easiest way to model insulators.

POLE LOCATION: Here are some common engineering practices to help you plan and construct a miniature pole line.

Hilly Terrain: Poles are located at the tops of rises and span narrow gullies and ravines. Where the distance is too great to span, poles will descend into the valley and then climb up the other side.

Direction Change: Wherever a change in direction greater than 45 degrees occurs, a "corner" is formed—a second crossarm faces the new destination, and the pole is braced with guy wires angling away from near its top down to ground anchors. This bracing offsets the inward pull of the new direction.

Tunnels: Communication lines are never placed in tunnels, but instead follow over the top of the hill. This is done to prevent the loss of communication in the event of a tunnel fire, wreck, or collapse.

Crossarms: On standard pole lines, crossarms on subsequent poles face opposite to each other, alternating from the front side to the back side of the pole.

Clearances: Wires crossing over highways or roads require a vertical separation of 18 feet. Those crossing railroad tracks require a 27-foot vertical separation to prevent snagging from oversize loads or equipment.

Guidelines: Follow these basic guidelines, and your railroad's pole lines will look as if they could really be carrying messages. Hmmmm; maybe if we . . . .

ABOVE: This illuminated switchstand is made from brass. Its green and red lenses indicate the position of the switch. LEFT: This switchstand, modified from a Grandt Line kit, doesn't turn, but it does light for effect.

SWITCHSTANDS

A variety of switchstand types can be bought, assembled, and painted to give switches the finishing touch. Most stands don't actually throw the switch, but they can be lighted, and they can be turned by switch machines so that either red or green indicates the position of the switch. We modified these older-style Grandt Line switchstands (part no. 3021) by drilling out the lamp housing, then inserting a 16-volt sub-mini bulb (Walthers no. 942-365) to light them. They don't turn but are very realistic when the room lights are dimmed. Again check all clearances so that switchstands placed on a curve don't get knocked over by the wide-swinging pilot or sidesill of a long passenger car taking the diverging route.

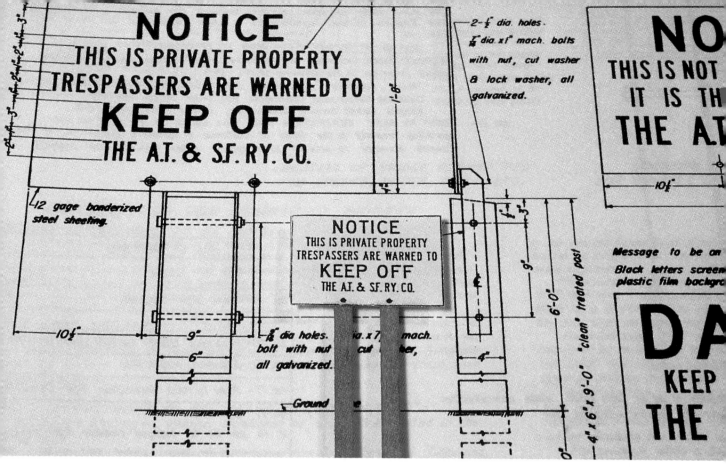

RIGHT-OF-WAY SIGNS

In 1978, Kachina Press of Dallas, Texas, came out with a series of three books titled *The Chief Way Reference Series,* subtitled *System Standards.* The books reprint AT&SF Railway engineering blueprints and schematics drawn by their draftsmen for just about every conceivable item on the railroad, from picks and shovels to roundhouses, turntables, bridges, depots, and almost every other railroad-related item you can imagine.

Volumes 1 and 2 contain excellent representations of signposts generic to almost any railroad, while others are purely Santa Fe and perfect for reproduction on the JL/ATSF Railway.

There's a simple technique for duplicating the signs you'll need for your O scale railroad. Simply take the book to a local printing and duplicating store and make a full-size copy of the signs you select. Then, using liquid correction fluid, paint out all drafting lines and construction instructions that get in the way of the reproduction.

Once this is done, use the standard reduction process on the copy machine to step down the sign to O scale. Cut the scale sign out of the paper reproduction, and glue it to a piece of .015" sheet styrene or cardstock cut to size. A strip of 1/8"-square balsa serves as the post, which should be colored with a walnut stain. Allow an extra 1/4" length for the post so you can glue it into a predrilled hole.

Signposts like these are required by all railroads. "Danger," "Close Clearance," and "No Trespassing" signs are common at bridges and tunnels as warnings to the public, as are an interesting variety of additional trackside signs for train crews.

OTHER DETAILS

There are other kinds of details, not usually associated with a railroad right-of-way, that really dress up a

Miniature signs can be made by photocopying prototype blueprints. Placed on the layout, the signs faithfully duplicate prototype information.

Some details are geospecific. Take oil wells, for instance; they're everywhere in Southern California. Boomtown Models makes this operating model. The dog, man, wooden fence, and oil spills don't come with the kit.

layout. An oil pump, for example. Oil derricks and oil pumps can be seen all over Southern California. In the early part of the century when wood wasn't considered scarce enough to conserve, oil derricks were constructed from wood and left standing erect.

By the 1940s and the development of portable derricks, it became cost-effective to dismantle the derrick tower and leave just the pump. Boomtown Models (Dallas, Texas) offers a terrific working pump for O scale; it should be placed toward the front of the layout, where all its detail can be appreciated. In California, it's not unusual to see pumps like these in the middle of some towns and cities. In the accompanying photo, a wooden fence keeps folks at a safe distance yet close enough to get a good look. We've blended the pump's base into the ground cover and dabbed a little fresh oil (glossy

black paint) here and there nearby. A local citizen and his dog are curious onlookers.

LET THERE BE LIGHT!

In your darkened layout room, is there anything more beautiful than miniature lights illuminating passing trains? Unfortunately, creating realistic lights has been troublesome in the past; and depending on the era you're modeling, it can be even worse than troublesome.

Whatever the era, though, we've observed that in all cities, towns, and villages, electric lights are mounted on wooden poles. Sometimes the same poles have been used for decades, and only the lamp and fixture have been brought up to date. In the 1930s, '40s, and '50s, a common light source for most streets was the standard pole and reflector, rarely protected by any type of glass cover. These lights can be modeled

Signals

Prototype signals tell the engineer whether his train can occupy a section of track. If that section contains a switch or crossing, the signal indication will also interlock with that junction to confirm its condition. Signals, as such, convey information vital to the safe movement of the rail transportation system. Many of them can be modeled to enhance operation and increase realism. Here are some common signal types you may wish to consider.

BLOCK SIGNALS: Whether interlocking or not, block signals indicate the condition of the track ahead. This always applies to occupancy, but can include a defective or broken rail and, connected to electronic fence detectors, rock or snow slides.

Signal heads (the casing that contains mechanisms and bulbs) and faces (the signal front with roundel lenses facing the track) are mounted on signal masts, bridges (if they're over multiple tracks), or cantilevers (inverted L-shape spanning single or double tracks) designed to maximize their visibility. Modern mainline block signal types commonly used are:

Color light—with three roundels (lenses) displayed vertically on the signal face indicating green-amber-red (top to bottom).

Searchlight—using a single bulb and roundel system to project three colors on the signal's face

Position light—with eight roundels placed in a circle on the signal face and a ninth in the center. Found primarily on Eastern railroads, the single fog-penetrating amber color indication is displayed in rows of three or more roundels.

Semaphore—the counterbalanced movable blade (arm) supplemented by green-amber-red roundels illuminated by one bulb. The blade of the lower-quadrant type moves from a 60° downward angle and green indication, to a 45° downward amber indication, to a 90° horizontal red indication. Conversely, the blade of the upper-quadrant type moves from green at the vertical down

through amber at the 45°, down to red at the 90° horizontal. Few lower-quadrant types remain in service, but upper-quadrant semaphores are still in use on portions of the Santa Fe Railway's main line in the southwest.

DWARF SIGNALS: As the name implies, these are short signals used most commonly in yards where close clearances are the rule. Interestingly, they can be of any of the block-signal types.

TRAIN ORDER SIGNALS: Relics of a bygone era preceding radio communication and automated signaling, train order signals were usually located at depots where they were manually operated by the agent on duty. Having received a telegraph (or phone) communication from the district's dispatcher, the agent would set the blade of the semaphore-like signal to either a vertical green (no orders), a 45° amber (pick up Form 19 on-the-fly), or horizontal red (stop for Form 31, a restrictive order needing signed acknowledgment from the crew).

SIGNAL INDICATIONS AND ASPECTS: A complexity reduced here to generality. Signal indications convey an action to be taken ("proceed," for example) while displaying an aspect ("green") having a name ("clear"), but the simplicity of this concept doesn't cover all contingencies. These contingencies are governed by operating rules in the employees' timetable, which states in detail which rules are in effect where.

For the modeler interested in using signals as basic traffic lights, simple signal indications and aspects are best kept to:

Clear—green aspect

Proceed (with caution/slow speed)—amber aspect

Stop—red aspect

CONTROL: Indications can be controlled by a variety of electronic devices currently available, some using optical sensors, and others detection circuits or relays. Or you can control them manually by turning toggle switches on or off.

Fig. 8-3 (RIGHT). Materials needed to make a lamp-post are a 12-volt grain-of-wheat bulb, a lampshade, and a dowel.

Fig. 8-4 (BELOW). Distress the lamp-post dowel with a razor saw.

Fig. 8-5 (BOTTOM). Use a motor tool to slot the dowel lengthwise, and use super glue to hold the bulb wires in place.

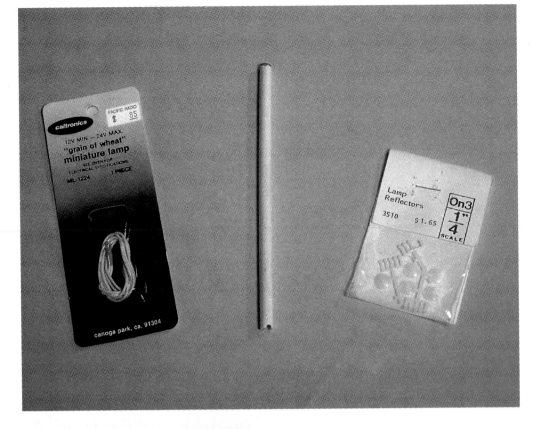

and then placed all over your layout.

A realistic lamp size with good intensity is the 12-volt grain-of-wheat bulb available from Radio Shack. The JL/ATSF uses dozens of these bulbs. And lighting them with only 9 volts ensures their surviving for years. It's a good idea to use toggle switches to turn groups of lights on or off, because all lights don't turn on simultaneously in real life.

Start with a package of 12-volt grain-of-wheat bulbs, a ¼" diameter wooden dowel, and a package of O scale lampshades, available from several detail company sources; we used Grandt Line part no. 3510 and Berkshire Valley part no. 551, for example. Figure 8-3 shows the components needed to build a JL/ATSF-style lamp post.

Cut the wooden dowel into 4" lengths; in O scale that would be 16 feet. The pigtails from the grain-of-wheat bulbs are long enough to run the length of the dowel with enough left over to pass through the table to accessory power bus wires beneath it. Distress the dowel for a realistic wood-grain effect. To do this, use a razor saw blade and scrape the dowel vertically, turning it in your hand as you draw the blade along its length, as shown in fig. 8-4.

With a motor tool and cutting disk, carefully groove the dowel along its entire length (fig. 8-5). This groove will route the pigtails from the lamp and must be deep and wide enough to accommodate them. Thread the pigtails through the lamp reflector, and touch the opening in the reflector with a drop of super glue to fix it to the bulb. Now paint the inside of the reflector white and the top of the reflector black or dark green. When the paint has dried, bend the top of the pigtails (with the bulb and reflector attached) to a natural curve. Next, glue the pigtails into the groove in the dowel. Color the dowel with Floquil Walnut Stain, then paint the pigtails, fig. 8-6, with Floquil Grimy Black to make them look like conduits.

You can use the bulb and reflector by themselves for a variety of other applications. Assemble them in the same way without the dowel and attach them to buildings by simply drilling a hole in the wall, then threading the pigtails out of sight inside the structure. When appropriately placed, they cast a very realistic light.

Your imagination and observation, whether in the field or out of books, can continually challenge your ability to reproduce the details all around you in real life. It's a good idea to bring a camera along on outings to capture a particular detail from several angles. Then when it's time to model it, you'll have done the research and are ready to have fun!

Fig. 8-6. Paint the dowel and the bulb leads to simulate electrical conduit.

With the room lights down, the lamppost nicely illuminates the Lionel operating milk car's platform.

9 Mini-Scenes

ONE WOULD THINK the primary interest a visitor would have when visiting the layout would be to see trains running. Not so; they're usually attracted to the scenery and "mini-scenes," and they're amazed by the look of a fully scenicked and detailed miniature world! After several minutes, you ask, kind of apologetically, "Would you like to see the trains run, too?"

Building a layout is a fun and leisurely activity. It would be difficult to think of all the hours and labor required to design and build it as anything other than an adventure you look forward to each time you return to its construction. When it came time for us to pay attention to creating mini-scenes, we had lots of fun as we went about positioning people, animals, so-called "hand props," and a myriad of details to give life to a specific place on the layout. It's these mini-scenes that a visitor will invariably focus on and comment, "How neat; that's just like the real thing!"

THE CIRCLE L RANCH

A mini-scene is a visual short story—let your imagination run wild. Here's an example. The Circle L Ranch, shown in the photo at left, consists of a ranch house, a barn, an old cabin, and grazing land with cattle, a few horses, tractors, a watering hole, and water pump.

Just gathering and grouping the cattle is a story by itself. It was tough finding cattle that were the right scale, let alone a variety of cows, bulls, steers, and calves either grazing or lying down. Business trips turned into time spent poking around in train and toy stores until the right size animals (made by a firm in Germany) turned up. The train store had only a limited selection, so we contacted the importer. The importer put us in touch with the manufacturer in Germany, and finally through written correspondence, we were able to buy the cattle and horses we wanted for the ranch.

But there's more to the story. When the package arrived, inside was everything we had ordered—plus several bison! A letter to the company got us this explanation. Since they had only two bulls to send us and thought the bison looked like bulls, they sent them along to fill out the order. This explains why there are a couple of bison milling around with the cattle in this mini-scene, and it's not just another bull story!

Grouping animals logically also adds realism to the scene. We've placed the calves near the cows, while the steers graze elsewhere. The imported cattle are indigenous to Germany, so we gave each of them a Hereford "white face" paint scheme and at the same time branded them with the Circle L (Lesser) Ranch brand. Herefords, as you probably know, are hardy beef cattle that are raised extensively in the western U.S.

If you look closely at the photo of the ranch house, you'll pick out another domestic scene. In the front yard, kids are playing as Uncle Charlie drives up in his "woody" station wagon to visit. Mrs. Wood greets him as he gets out of the car.

Does this animal look like a bull? There is logic right down to the placement of cows, steers, and heifers, and that's no bull. Did you spot the Circle L brand? Gee, that looks somehow familiar.

The Wood kids just keep playing as Mrs. Wood greets Charlie. He has evidently dropped by for a visit in the Whispering Pines Resort's "woody."

A Santa Fe pickup truck sits parked alongside the Highland Junction Tower. It's been repainted, decaled, and sprayed with Dullcote. Spend a couple of minutes checking out all the details in this 12" x 15" mini-scene.

In 1986, relatively few "little people" were realistically painted, and most were shiny with some kind of molded base to stand on. Most figures were still being made for temporary setups. By 1988, far more realistic figures became available in stores and catalogs, and these "little people" had more natural poses, interesting implied action, and no bases. We're partial to the figures made by Dennis DiBattista, whose company, Arttista Accessories, regularly adds new figures to its catalog at a modest price. A simple paint wash of flat black diluted with Dio-Sol brings out facial and clothing details realistically. If necessary, a light spray of Testor's Dullcote flattens any shine.

HIGHLAND JUNCTION TOWER

Here's how we made an ordinary scene into an attention-getter. We started out with a readily available Solido Models 1950 Dodge pickup truck—other brands will do as well. After checking photographs, we found the correct yellow color and appropriate Santa Fe decal for the herald decoration. We covered the truck's windows with masking tape and gave the truck a coat of Floquil Armour Yellow, being careful not to paint the radiator, headlights, or wheels. Once this dried, we applied the Santa Fe herald (a Champ decal) and a light wash of Floquil Engine Black diluted with Dio-Sol and dabbed it onto the radiator, headlights, and wheel rims.

The final step was to spray the truck with Dullcote. Be sure to use Dullcote in a well-ventilated area, and take appropriate precautions (rubber gloves, respirator mask); its fumes are quite strong.

A tower operator is on his way out when a visitor appears on his motorcycle, and he waves to him. The tower road is dirt and gravel; it makes an interesting contrast to the paved road. While the tower road was drying, we rolled the truck over the still-wet dirt, creating tread marks and also mucking up the truck's tires, adding another touch of realism. Other details in this 12" x 15" mini-scene are dwarf and searchlight signals, cactus around the base of the tower, a signal shed, and a whistle/station signpost. Mini-scene details, as demonstrated here, should be logical and carefully integrated. It's even better if you can make them tell a story!

THE PLAZA

We're all familiar with these typical scenes in a small town plaza. Along the walkways there are benches, birds, maybe a drinking fountain, and people. Here people feed the birds while another person watches. Don't forget the birdseed! A few grains of fine sand make excellent birdseed. Depending on what other figures you like, there can be a man getting his shoes shined, a gardener mowing the lawn, picnic tables, kids playing, a bicycle propped against a lamppost, and other vignettes limited only by your imagination—and figure availability, of course.

2:30 p.m. . . . Where's Johnson? . . . Late again? Here he comes running, as always, with a good excuse for being late. Oh well, in a couple hours it'll be dinner time, and he'll run over to Pete & Joe's Diner. Wonder what their blue-plate special is tonight? . . .

Just another day in the Plaza feeding the pigeons, getting the shoes shined, and watching the grass grow. Wonder when the band will show up?

ABOVE: Plenty of activity in downtown Molino. Charlie's late for an appointment, and the mailman's trying to make his appointed rounds. Fido's doing a better job of impeding him than rain, sleet, or snow could ever do.

RIGHT: Could that be Elvis in the rumble seat? Guess it could be; it's only the late 1940s in Molino. Even the dog has done his part to detail the scene.

Probably meatloaf again. Oh, oh. There's the postman making his rounds with Fido nipping at his pants as usual.

Look! There's Elvis sitting in the rumble seat of his spiffy car, carrying on with Clara. Her dog could care less. He's got his own business to take care of. Oops, watch where you step! That guy's checking his watch. Maybe he's waiting for Johnson to show up.

The imaginative story continues, stimulated by the mini-scene's visuals. Not all of the figures shown in these photos were available at the same time, but whenever we came across new ones we tried to imagine how they'd look in a scene. That's how the JL/ATSF Railway population forever keeps on growing!

Sometimes mini-scenes are at some distance from the front of the layout, but that's no excuse for leaving an area void of activity. As we completed the layout zones, we concluded each with its own group of mini-scenes. In order to see the more distant ones, we have a small pair of binoculars on hand to give visitors a wonderful close-up look. Interestingly, viewed through the binoculars, everything surrounding the mini-scene is blocked out, and you almost get the feeling of being a part of it. It's fun! Try it yourself. Most sporting goods stores have a wide selection of inexpensive, good-quality binoculars.

ROAD CONSTRUCTION AHEAD

One of the unique mini-scenes on the JL/ATSF is built entirely on top of an access hatch. Here was a chance to use some tractors to make road improvements just a few yards away from the Cucamonga Depot. It's a two-lane road with one lane torn up to have a new coat of asphalt applied. The construction crew had to break up the old surface and then grade it level. A flagman at each end of the construction area slows the traffic and protects the workers. They've set up barricades at either end of the site. A prototypical "danger" lantern by the barricade actually lights at night. Two tractors are on the job. The grader has had its cab removed and been dirtied up to make it more realistic. The steam roller is also appropriate for the era.

Jack's out there shoveling dirt while Bob, the "super," looks on—his hands, of course, in his pockets. Just off to the side on the embankment are the men's lunch pails and thermos bottles. Extra hand tools are lying around for the rest of the crew when they get back to work. Different ground covers (i.e., dirt, old road-graded dirt, and a new layer of asphalt) add to the realism. When the access hatch is lowered, the entire mini-scene drops out of sight.

Think of all the possible stories that can be told about mini-scenes on a layout! Like searching for pieces of a puzzle, it's really fun to find people and props to tell those stories.

Near Cucamonga Station the highway is being repaved. Many details are incorporated in this typical mini-scene, including a barricade, lantern, and flagman to alert drivers of the road construction ahead. This particular mini-scene is glued securely on top of the access hatch. When it's lowered not a grain of dirt falls off.

10 Building a Town

ANYTOWN, U.S.A. You've seen it on TV, or you've visited it, or maybe you were even born and raised in it. Regardless of your experience with small towns, when you get right down to it, every small town has similar buildings, streets, and parks. Yet each town retains its own identity or personality, and it's that look we want to duplicate with our model towns. If your experience with small towns is limited, consider taking a Sunday afternoon drive. Be sure to take along your camera and a note pad so you can document the details

you see. You'll be surprised how long your list is! It's many of these elements that you'll want to include in your modeling.

Although the variety of structure kits is somewhat limited in O scale, available kits can be customized and then combined to bring business to the small town plaza. On the JL/ATSF Railway the town's name is Molino. Such a town existed in the early 1900s east of Pasadena, California. As we noted in the first paragraph, all little towns are basically alike, so what follows is a description of how we built a town; use our experience and techniques to guide you as you build your own version of Anytown, U.S.A.

STREETS AND CURBS

The best way to begin construction is to complete the planned buildings first so you can see how they'll best fit into the overall space. An integral part of placing them is determining how the streets will bisect. When you feel you have the best arrangement, cut out pieces of cardboard about the scale width of a street (approximately 22 scale feet or 5½").

Position the cut-out templates and mark their outline on the plywood. Next, using 1/16"-thick sheet balsa, cut pieces to match the lines marked for the streets. We also cut balsa for the depot parking lot and the gas station

UPPER LEFT: Street layout is critical in establishing believability. The zone in which Molino Plaza and depot were to be built began with pieces of cardboard cut to the scale width of a street, allowing the right amount of space for structures.

LOWER LEFT: Cracks and tar seams were added to the streets with a fine-point Sharpie permanent marker. A light wash of diluted Floquil Weathered Black does a nice job of aging the concrete streets.

service area, since they are all part of the street plan and will be painted the same color. Glue the balsa pieces to the plywood. The streets should be wide enough for at least single-lane, two-way traffic, plus space for parking on one or both sides of the street. A lot of space is necessary for streets, but they'll look realistic when cars and trucks are placed on them.

The actual streets modeled will determine their color and how they'll be finished. Lightly sand the balsa and use spackle-type filler to smooth any seams. Then apply a coat of sanding sealer (available at model airplane hobby shops), which seals the porous balsa and makes it easier to paint, in this case with Floquil Concrete. Add cracks and potholes for realism. A fine-point Sharpie permanent marker works well to draw cracks or tar seams. If your town is going to have sidewalks, then you'll want to make

curbs and raise the buildings and other structures a little higher than the streets. Strips of ⅛"-thick balsa cut to fit work well for the curbs. Manhole covers (Chooch Enterprises Inc., part no. 5163) and a light wash of diluted Floquil Weathered Black (1 part paint, 20 parts Dio-Sol) puddled on with an eyedropper can be added to simulate concrete streets.

GRADE CROSSINGS

Consider the location of grade crossings (where streets and tracks intersect). The major crossing in Molino is at a point where the main railroad line and main street leading in and out of the town meet. Besides the expected railroad crossing signs and street markings, a pair of scratchbuilt wig-wag signals warn motorists. They light up, wag, and have a synchronized bell-ringing sound system! The same street crosses the tracks and

Flashing crossbucks, crossing gates, and a ringing-bell sound system protect motorists at this busy railroad crossing.

continues to another part of town. At this grade crossing, gates and flashing crossbucks are appropriate. The crossbucks are modified NJ International signals with scratchbuilt crossing gates raised and lowered by Tortoise motors. These signals also have a tied-in sound system. Leading away from the business district, the concrete street becomes a dirt service road for Young's Coal Company. Prototypically, wooden planks are fastened between the rails for vehicular traffic crossing the tracks. A lead pencil point pressed into the planks simulates bolt heads that hold the planks in place.

THE PLAZA

Towns dating back to the early 1900s usually have a central plaza. We modeled Molino's plaza after the one in Las Vegas, New Mexico. A curb surrounds the model Molino plaza. This rise above the street matches the height of the walkways crisscrossing it. A scratchbuilt typical gazebo sits in the middle of the park.

TOP: The gazebo in its town plaza helps to capture the unique identity of Molino. The plaza at Las Vegas, New Mexico, was a source of reference for the Molino plaza. Scale lampposts are difficult to find. N.J. International's had to be modified, but the size and era are correct. ABOVE: This statue of a man holding aloft a huge Lionel track pin is dedicated to the honor of Pete and Joe's hero, the legendary Mr. Leo Nell.

Scenic imitation grass mat material on a paper backing is available in rolls (Faller, imported by Walthers). Pieces of grass-paper are cut to fill spaces between cement walkways and street curbs. Lampposts and lights should be installed at this stage

Molino Depot is an accurate reproduction of a typical turn-of-the-century Santa Fe station. A realistic depot loading platform should service at least two or three passenger car lengths.

too. We used lampposts available from NJ International; with some modification they fit in perfectly with the era of the JL/ATSF Railway. The modification involves the removal of the metal, disklike bases that came with the lampposts; they now enhance the freight yard junk pile. The palm trees are professionally produced trees for architectural modeling, available from a local hobby shop. All the other trees were assembled at a "tree party," at which a bunch of us sat around the breakfast table and made trees. Working with tree armatures, i.e., skeletons selected from twigs of actual bushes, we attached Woodland Scenics Foliage material with dabs of white glue. Who can say they don't look like real trees?

Other details of the plaza have been added over time. For example, a variety of "little people," bicycles, pigeons, picnic tables, and the not-to-be-missed heroic statue of Leo Nell, holding aloft a huge track pin—a touch of whimsical humor. We're still looking for an O scale municipal band for the gazebo.

BUILDINGS SURROUNDING THE PLAZA

Across the street from the plaza is the Molino depot. While researching the prototype town, we located a photo of the Molino station in around 1910 and were struck by its similarity to Lionel's Freight Station Kit 6-2787. Painting the station the actual mineral brown color of Santa Fe stations at the early part of the century;

adding details such as signs, a weather vane, and window shades; and extending the loading platform alongside the track all enhance realism. The station platform is built to the height of the tracks and extends around the entire structure so that steps from the parking lot add another interesting bit of detail. The train order signal is a combination of parts from NJ International signals kitbashed, activated by a Tortoise slow-motion motor mounted beneath the table. Train-order signals haven't been used for many years, having been replaced by radio communication. Neither of us is aware of a commercially available O gauge signal of this type.

The Texaco service station, described in Chapter 7, is a slightly modified K-Line kit. Fortunately, the Texaco public relations office in White Plains, New York, does a good job of maintaining public relations. They promptly answered our request for any visual help they could provide to show what Texaco stations looked like in the late 1940s and early '50s. The photographs they sent confirmed

that the K-Line station had in fact been designed after these early gas stations. In addition to photographs, the company also supplied us with logos that we used to make the prototypical mast sign. Colors and other signs were also copied from the photographs. With the building in place, added details (from Selley and Berkshire Valley) really give the gas station a lifelike appearance.

Pete & Joe's Diner looked pretty good assembled straight from the box, but we decided it would look even better if we elevated it above the "street level" so it could be seen from 6 feet

Pete & Joe's Diner, home of the famous Blue Plate (not fishplate) Special, is elevated above the street to make it more visible from a distance.

Photos of small towns in the 1940s and '50s show how prevalent was the use of canvas awnings. Some were later replaced by metal ones.

away. It also became a compact view-block for the tracks behind it. Another K-Line kit, the diner can be bought for $10 or less, and dressing it up with signs depicting prices of the 1950s, plus adding the outdoor walk-around railings and steps give it a look totally different from the out-of-the-box plastic kit.

The Design Preservation Models (DPM) kits used for the bank and office building are finely detailed. We had to relocate the corner entrance to better fit the town's overall design. After studying photographs of towns from the 1940s, we added the awning. It's a nice touch. We took individual window measurements to draw the awning outlines on a sheet of .015" styrene. Using pinking shears, we then cut out the triangle pattern borders of typical canvas awnings. Super glue secures the edges and attaches the awning to the building.

Small three-dimensional plastic letters are available in artist and drafting supply stores. They can be used for a variety of applications. For example, town and city buildings are sometimes named after the builder or perhaps a benefactor. We named one of our

structures the Walker Building in honor of Chard L. Walker, a longtime employee of the Santa Fe Railway and operator/telegrapher for more than 12 years at the former Summit station at the top of Cajon Pass.

We decided not to locate any tall structures along the front of the layout, since they would only block the view of Molino. Instead, as was typical of many California towns, a roadside fruit stand (a kit by Selley) occupies a spot along the road. Two nearby orange trees, laden with fruit made from decorative glass beads painted and glued to the trees, shade a bunch of other details that complete this mini-scene.

An oil pump adjacent to the orange trees is appropriate too. This motorized pump kit is available from Boomtown Models of Dallas, Texas. It's the type of accessory that can be used for several scales because the prototype exists in many sizes. Protecting it with a fence and "little people" and a set of Burma-Shave rural highway signs completes the Molino Plaza area.

BELIEVABLE CHARACTER

It's our belief that Hi-railers' approach to modeling a town should be to create the essence of believable character. Streets, curbs, and sidewalks must be of acceptable width, and buildings should be realistically spaced. You can even have a few empty lots. Finally, the selection and placement of details and of "little people" creates realism, a sense of activity, and a lived-in feeling.

Since the building of your town will most likely come near the end of the layout-building process, you still have plenty of time to gather details and photos. Break out the camera, grab a pencil and tablet, and head out for Anytown, U.S.A. It's just down the road a ways.

A nice variety of fresh fruit from the farm (and Coke) is what Jo Ann sells every day of the week. Roadside stands like this were—and, to a lesser extent, still are—common along California's highways and roads.

11 Hi-Railing Toward Realism

A FINE LINE SEPARATES the scale modeler from the O gauge Hi-railer. In fact, it's not really a line at all; it's a third rail. But that third rail is a "given" for us Hi-railers, and it doesn't bother most of us. It's something we've grown up with and most of us don't even notice any more. "Third rail? What third rail? Oh, *that* third rail!" In some ways it's become a badge of honor: "Three-rail track and proud of it!"

Yet in every other way, we Hi-railers would like our trains and layouts to be just as scalelike as we can make them. And there are more and more scale toy trains coming to the market. The two largest train manufacturers, Lionel and K-Line, still produce toy trains proportioned to the classic O gauge, smaller-than-scale size, but they've also produced some excellent O scale items. Other manufacturers, such as Williams, Right-Of-Way,

Is it scale, or is it Hi-rail? Hard to tell without seeing that third rail, isn't it? Gee, if that's the only difference, what's all the scale vs. toy fuss about?

91

Not too many O gauge Santa Fe-prototype steam engines have been manufactured; Eastern roads—especially the Pennsy—have dominated the market. Unless you're a real purist, though, it doesn't really matter. Paint her up, add a few Santa Fe details and an ATSF herald, and call it "close enough."

Weaver, and M.T.H., cater almost exclusively to the Hi-railers, and they've seen significant growth in this segment of the O market. Until relatively recently we could browse through catalogs of O gauge trains and buy the few items that were appropriate for a Hi-rail layout. Today we have a tough time choosing which items we want to buy. Even if you could limit your purchases to one prototype railroad, such as the Santa Fe in our case, you'd find this by itself would represent a pretty costly expenditure.

BACK TO THE PROTOTYPE

The Hi-railer should realize that real railroads have always customized the equipment they order from builders. They implement special modifications depending on the geography of their

right-of-way, the special operation requirements of their trains and various personal technical preferences. It's like buying a basic car and then adding this or that option.

Hi-rail manufacturers still bet on major markets for their prototype steam locomotive models, and their favorite is the Pennsylvania in almost every case. With few exceptions, it's still difficult to get a steam locomotive that's truly prototypical for the Santa Fe. The more common locomotives such as Mikado, Pacific, Consolidation, and Hudson types that most railroads operated were individually modified by the builder for that particular railroad. On the JL/ATSF Railway, we have examples of each of these different types of steam locomotives and have modified them to approximate Santa Fe prototypes. But often the design of the boiler, steam dome, sandbox, firebox even the cab, are not of Santa Fe type, and to change the brass or die-cast construction is no easy job. Even the tenders almost always have coal loads, which again isn't, with some exceptions, prototypical for the Santa Fe.

If the truth were known, we don't really care much that a particular locomotive doesn't match the prototype exactly. The modifications we've made are pleasing, and the lighted number boards are specifically Santa Fe, with numbers accurately corresponding to the particular prototype locomotive class. Look at the world of difference these recent models make when they look prototypical!

Another philosophical change is occurring. The "collector" mania for these new models is almost nonexistent. Perhaps, as John Grams noted in his *Classic Toy Trains* magazine article (October 1991), it was what he called "the nostalgia market" that mostly created the demand, which affects the supply, and which in turn determines the market price of classic toy train collectibles. These newer trains don't have that "nostalgia" baggage attached to them.

The Hi-railer, unlike the collector, buys a particular locomotive for no other reason than to run it. Why then shouldn't he also weather a locomotive that would have been in service on the prototype for 20 or 30 years? Maybe not a well-maintained streamliner, but certainly a freight yard switcher for realism's sake. And that

ABOVE: Now that scale-body freight cars are being offered at reasonable prices, operators shouldn't worry too much about weathering freight cars to look like the real ones.

LEFT: This Madison-type passenger car has been repainted and decaled for use as a maintenance-of-way sleeping car on the JL/ATSF Railway.

A Santa Fe RDC car, kitbashed from a pair of Lionel Budd cars in less-than-perfect shape, proudly displays its Warbonnet-heritage paint scheme.

carries over to rolling stock. The same criteria apply, only freight cars are less specific to any one particular railroad, and many currently produced models are excellent generic scale reproductions. As greater varieties of cars, consecutively numbered in paint schemes for more railroads, become available, they beg to be weathered to look like the real ones! Since there seems to be no reason for these modern trains to become collectible, why not do what we want with them and not concern ourselves with what their value may or may not be in the future?

Here's an idea whose time may be right. At every train meet there are literally thousands of O gauge cars that never were collectibles. They are so numerous they can be purchased for less than $20. Many times, however, a car the collector thinks of as "junker" or perhaps as a current-production car with no collectible value, is the same car the Hi-railer sees as

one with a future. Take that Williams passenger car, strip it, repaint it, and decal it to look like a maintenance-of-way car no manufacturer has offered. It may not be exactly scale, but it sure will look great on your layout. And the beauty of it all is that these gems in the rough are plentiful!

A superb example (even though it cost considerably more than a junker freight car) are the Santa Fe RDC cars we kitbashed. Some years ago, one of the toy train club magazines published an article by Jack Whitmeyer. In it he described how he took two Lionel Budd cars, cut them apart, and combined the pieces to make a more prototypical single car wearing the red-nosed Santa Fe paint scheme. A set of three of these Lionel cars showed up at a local train meet wearing a very reasonable price tag. Since they would be kitbashed the RDCs didn't have to be in mint condition; upon close inspection, it became clear the reason the set was available and reasonably priced was that it was rather beaten-up. Turning the units into a prototypically correct RDC involved major surgery and a lot of hard work, but the results justified the effort.

THE FUTURE OF HI-RAILING

Today, the Hi-railer's desire to achieve better operation of his model trains, greater realism in every aspect of his layout, and modular layouts where he can run prototypical-length trains with lashups and double-heading, are all attainable realities.

Model trains are getting better and better looking as a result of competition between manufacturers; this same competition has resulted in improved locomotive performance, better-looking track and switches, remotely controlled couplers, profuse smoke, you-are-there sound effects, and other amazing features.

In addition to competition, another factor that has strongly affected the hobby is modern technology from the non-hobby world. Sophisticated electronics, highly detailed accurate plastic extrusions, incredible miniature sound chips, colorful and prototypical computer graphics that imprint superior looking cars, and general state-of-the-art production methodology are all part of the manufacturers' ability to give us the best model trains we've ever had.

And it's great to know that Lionel Trains—the preeminent manufacturer of toy trains and supplier for many of us of our very first train—is leading the industry again with its exciting new TrainMaster system! While the concept of radio-controlled walkaround throttles may not be new for HO trains, in O gauge and particularly for us Hi-railers, this innovative system from Lionel is phenomenal. We've begun using it on the JL/ATSF, together with Rail-

sounds II. We can turn off the room lights and keep on just the layout lights. With the mood thus established, operating a Railsounds II diesel with the CAB-1 Wireless Remote Control is the ultimate! And we're told it's just the beginning! Our senses return to our prototype experiences—sound echoes heard at the famous Sullivan Curve on the Santa Fe Railway near Cajon Pass. Just close your eyes and listen to those growling diesels, not yet in sight, climbing toward the Curve. All of these sounds are now possible with Railsounds II.

And the Lionel TrainMaster frees us from arm's-length reach of fixed cab and throttle controls. The Hi-railer may now well discover new layout designs in which he'll actually walk beside his trains as they roll along from town to town. In any case, the Hi-railer isn't going to be satisfied until within his three-rail domain trains run with superior precision and his layout and trains duplicate the real thing as closely as possible.

The potential is limitless. . . . Hi-railing in the future is going to be a great ride!

Here's hoping you hop aboard the Hi-rail line with Joe and Pete. It's going to be a great ride!

95

Selected Hi-Rail Suppliers
and Related Products Manufacturers

Arttista
1616 S. Franklin St.
Philadelphia, PA 19148
Hand-painted action figures

Berkshire Valley Models
P. O. Box 150
Adams, MA 01220
Detail parts and buildings

Boomtown Models
P. O. Box 181774
Dallas, TX 75218
Oil pumps, cactus

Bowser Mfg. Co.
21 Howard St.
P. O. Box 322
Montoursville, PA 17754-0322
Handpainted figures, turntables

Buildings Unlimited
P. O. Box 239
Nazareth, PA 18064-0239
Buildings, railroad structures

Castle Studio
175 Fifth Ave, Suite 2674
New York, NY 10010
Street signs

Champion Decal Co.
P. O. Box 1178
Minot, ND 58702
Decals

Chooch Enterprises, Inc.
P. O. Box 217
Redmond, WA 98052
Detail parts

Circuitron, Inc.
P. O. Box 322
Riverside, IL 60546
Electronic products

Classic Toy Trains Magazine
21017 Crossroads Circle
P. O. Box 1612
Waukesha, WI 53187
The leading magazine for toy train collectors and operators

Crown Model Products
484 Winter St.
Holliston, MA 01746,
Rolling stock

CTT, Inc.
109 Medallion Center
Dallas, TX 75214
Track-design templates

Curtis Hi-Rail Products, Inc.
P. O. Box 385
North Stonington, CT 06359
Switches, track and accessories

Dallee Electronics
10 Witmer Rd.
Lancaster, PA 17602
Electronic controllers, whistles

Depotronics, Inc.
P. O. Box 2093
Warrendale, PA 15086
Electronic controllers

Design Preservation Models
P. O. Box 66
Linn Creek, MO 65052
Building kits

Dremel Mfg. Co.
4915 21st St.
Racine, WI 53406
Motor tools

Floquil-Polly S Color Corp.
Rt. 30 N.
Amsterdam, NY 12010
Paints

GarGraves Trackage Corp.
Rt. 1 Box 255A
North Rose, NY 14516
Switches and track

Grandt Line Products
1040-B Shary Ct.
Concord, CA 94518
Switchstands, detail parts

Highball Products Co.
P. O. Box 43633
Cincinnati, OH 45243
Track ballast

House of Balsa
10101 Yucca Road
Adelanto, CA 92301
Tuf-Grind

Kalmbach Publishing Co./ Greenberg Books Division
21017 Crossroads Circle
P. O. Box 1612
Waukesha, WI 53187
Model railroading books and magazines

K.B.'s Die-cast Direct
1009 Twilight Trail
Frankfort, KY 40601
Automobiles, trucks, tractors

Keil Line Models
6440 McCullom Lake Rd.
Wonder Lake, IL 60097
Signals, detail parts

K-Line Electric Trains
P. O. Box 2831
Chapel Hill, NC 27515
Locomotives, rolling stock, accessories

Lexington Miniatures
P. O. Box 91
Lexington, IL 61753
Picnic benches, shelters, pallets

Lionel Trains, Inc.
50625 Richard W. Boulevard
Chesterfield, MI 48051-2493
Locomotives, rolling stock, accessories

Mainline Modules
P. O. Box 21861
Chattanooga, TN 37421-1861
Vinyl roadbed

Microscale Industries, Inc.
P. O. Box 11950
Costa Mesa, CA 92627
Decals

Mike's Train House
9693-A Gerwig Lane
Columbia, MD 21046
Locomotives and rolling stock

Model Railroader Magazine
21017 Crossroads Circle
P. O. Box 1612
Waukesha, WI 53187
Leading model railroad magazine, serving all scales

Moondog Express
104 W. Ocean Ave.
Lompoc, CA 93436
Rubber ties, streets, track patterns

New England Car Shops
241 Crescent St. #19
Waltham, MA 02154
Rolling stock

NJ International, Inc.
77 W. Nicholai St.
Hicksville, NY 11801
Switch machines, signals

Oakridge Corp.
P. O. Box 247
Lemonte, IL 60439
Model RR supplies

Plastruct
1020 S. Wallace Place
City of Industry, CA 91748
Oil tanks, plastic structural details

Precision Scale Co.
3961 Highway 93 North
Stevensville, MT 59870
Detail parts

RGS Limited Edition Trains
184 N. Main St.
Scranton, PA 18518
Rolling stock

Right-Of-Way Industries
P. O. Box 13036
Akron, OH 44313
Signals, rolling stock, locomotives

Ross Custom Switches
P. O. Box 110
North Stonington, CT 06359
Switches, track, and accessories

SamTech
6436 Mellow Wine Way
Columbia, MD 21044
Parts for Williams and upgrades

Selley Finishing Touches
21 Howard St.
Montoursville, PA 17754-0322
Detail accessories

Stevens International
P. O. Box 126
Magnolia, NJ 08049
Animals, people

Wm. K. Walthers Inc.
P. O. Box 18676
Milwaukee, WI 53218
Dwarf signals, RR supplies

Weaver Models
177 Wheatley Ave.
Northumberland, PA 17857
Rolling stock, locomotives

Williams Reproductions Ltd.
6660 Dobbin Rd.
Columbia, MD 21045
Locomotives and rolling stock

Woodland Scenics
P. O. Box 98
Linn Creek, MO 65052
Scenery materials